DATE DUE

JUN 0 9 2000	
JUL 1 7 2000	
JUL 1 1 2003	
SEP 1 1 2006	
OCT 15 2010	
NOV 2 2013	

PEOPLE
PLEASERS

Helping Others without Hurting Yourself

PEOPLE PLEASERS

Les Carter, PH.D.

BROADMAN
&HOLMAN
PUBLISHERS

Nashville, Tennessee

0-8054-2146-7

Published by Broadman & Holman Publishers, Nashville, Tennessee

Dewey Decimal Classification: 241
Subject Heading: HELPING BEHAVIOR—CHRISTIANITY / SELF-SACRIFICE
Library of Congress Card Catalog Number: 99-059090

Unless otherwise stated all Scripture citation is from the NASB, the New American Standard Bible, © the Lockman Foundation, 1960, 1962, 1963, 1968, 1971, 1972, 1973, 1975, 1977; used by permission. The other version cited is the NKJV, the New King James Version, copyright © 1979, 1980, 1982, Thomas Nelson, Inc., Publishers.

Library of Congress Cataloging-in-Publication Data

Carter, Les.
    People pleasers : helping others without hurting yourself / Les Carter.
       p. cm.
    ISBN 0-8054-2146-7 (HB)
    1. Helping behavior—Religious aspects—Christianity. 2. Self-sacrifice. I. Title.
BV4647.H4 C37 2000
241'.677—dc21

                                       99-059090
                                       CIP

1 2 3 4 5 04 03 02 01 00

Table of Contents

Foreword & Acknowledgments

Several years ago, I wrote a book called *Imperative People: Those Who Must Be In Control.* I had seen the devastating effects of controlling behavior upon relationships, so I wanted to draw attention to the fact that God never intended one person to control another. Instead, there are ways to create an atmosphere of influence and accountability that does not require people to resort to coercive or manipulative tactics. I found that many people apparently recognized imperative traits in themselves, and as a result, I have had the privilege of helping many make adjustments in this area.

As I conferred with people who have a strong controlling nature, my awareness of another pattern came more into focus. For every person who has control problems, there are several more people who cater to the controllers in a pattern of people pleasing. Just as the controlling pattern is unhealthy, I have seen that this people-pleasing pattern can be equally toxic. My desire, then, is to bring attention to the ways that people can be pleasing but without having to succumb to disrespectful or self-defeating behavior.

It is important to note that I fully believe in the necessity of such traits as servitude, kindness, and cooperation. Relationship healthiness depends heavily upon such foundational qualities. That said, I have found that many people overemphasize their compliance to the extent that they actually "encourage" others to continue manipulating and controlling them. What is worse, as the appeasing behavior remains imbalanced, these persons then experience ever-deepening struggles with resentment, fear, or false guilt. This pattern can and should be halted.

My aim in writing this book is to help people pleasers find balance between their desire to serve and their ability to be assertive. I operate on the assumption that no relationship unfolds without a few kinks, so it is necessary to know how to establish proper boundaries and resolve conflicts. People pleasers often assume they cannot afford to stand firmly for legitimate needs or convictions, but this is not the case. It is an act of love and responsibility when you correctly stand up for healthy convictions, or to put it in the reverse sense, you are doing no one any favors when you establish relationship patterns that perpetuate others' insensitivities.

As you read this book, approach it with a three-fold goal: Be willing to (1) identify the components in your relating style that are leading you in the wrong direction; (2) contemplate why you manage your life as you do; and (3) target healthy attitudes and behaviors that will lead to the desired improvements. To assist in these goals, at the end of each chapter, I have included questions called "For Personal Reflection." These are there to help you personalize the information in that chapter. If you choose to use these questions as part of a family or group discussion, that could certainly prove beneficial.

The case illustrations I use throughout the book are real, but I have been very careful to alter the identities of the persons involved to protect confidentiality. I am privileged to do the counseling work that I do, and I am grateful for the inspiration I receive from people who truly want to grow emotionally and spiritually.

Special thanks is due to Marti Miller for her fantastic assistance in preparing this manuscript. Not only is she a pleasant person, but she's efficient too. You can't beat that combination. Also I would like to thank Vicki Crumpton, Janis Whipple, Kim Overcash, and the rest of the staff at Broadman & Holman Publishers. I have been most pleased to be associated with this godly and competent staff.

Recognizing the People-Pleasing Pattern

Chapter 1

People Pleasing Is Not Always Pleasing

Somewhat sheepishly, Anita spoke with me as participants were going home from an Anger Workshop I had just completed. "I came here," she explained, "hoping to learn some things about the anger I see in both my husband and my father, but I'm leaving with a very different perspective of myself."

I had noticed on several occasions, as I taught the class of about thirty people, that Anita seemed steeped in thought. I knew the wheels had been turning in her mind, so I took the opportunity to probe. "Can I assume that you're having to admit that you struggle with anger too?"

"Yes, you certainly can assume that!" she replied emphatically. "You mentioned tonight how an angry person may not necessarily shout or slam doors or speak offensive words, but that it can be demonstrated through depression and withdrawal and chronic frustration. That's me! I'm so busy trying to figure out how to get along with people who have the more obvious forms of anger that I haven't really taken the time to recognize my own problem with anger."

We talked a few moments more; then Anita asked, "Could I schedule some individual appointments with you? I think there is quite a lot that we need to go over."

In the following weeks, I got to know Anita's story quite well, and I learned that her depression and frustrated emotions were actually the result of a long-standing pattern of people pleasing. "To say that my dad was strong-willed would be a polite understatement," she told me. "I was barely allowed to think an original thought because he was so opinionated that he wouldn't allow anyone to entertain ideas different from his. At a very early age, I became skilled at knowing how to gauge his mood and behave accordingly."

"Do you remember being angry, or did you ever rebel against his heavy-handedness?"

"Well, as a teenager, I guess you could say I had an attitude; at least that's what he told me. I would sneak around and do some drinking with my friends, but I would have died if he had caught me. So, yeah, I guess I had some rebellion; but mostly, I remember spending a lot of mental energy figuring out what I'd have to do to keep Dad happy. I learned, for instance, that if I kept things clean around the house or if I brought home good grades, he'd go a little easier on me. My younger brother constantly argued with him and it got him nowhere. Dad stayed chronically angry at him. I realized that compliance got me a lot less grief, so compliant I was!"

"What about your mother? Where was she through all of this?"

Anita shook her head gently. "Well, let's just say that she could be relatively easy to get along with when Dad wasn't around, but it all changed when he'd come onto the scene."

"What do you mean?"

"Take, for instance, an afternoon after school let out. Mom was usually pleasant until about six o'clock or so because that's when Dad would come home; then she'd turn into a different person. She'd gripe if my brother or I ever did anything to make him mad. She'd be tense, and it was almost as if she was afraid to be too friendly toward me because Dad might criticize her for it."

"So would it be safe to say that your mom had an unwritten rule that as soon as the Boss got home, everyone had to shut down their own uniqueness in order to keep peace?"

"Absolutely. I learned my compliance from the master teacher."

Now a mother of two in her mid-thirties, Anita had similar experiences with her husband, Ted. Though he wasn't the openly hostile person that her dad was, he was moody and not very attentive to her emotional needs. "I do everything I can to please Ted, but it never seems like he appreciates what I do for him. When I cook his favorite meal, you'd never know if he likes it because he's so stingy with compliments. Also, I bend over backwards keeping a clean house because that's what he wants, but I only hear about it if I *don't* do it right."

At the end of one session, I asked Anita to make a list of her compliant behaviors that seemed to go unappreciated by others. The next week she brought in thirty-eight examples! Among them were items like:

- Saturday morning I had to cancel plans to help at my best friend's garage sale because, at the last minute, my husband accepted an invitation to play golf, leaving me in charge of our five-year-old daughter.
- I bought two magazine subscriptions from a neighbor's son, even though I didn't need to be spending the money, because he said he had to get those sales for his class to win a special prize.
- Even though I don't think it's necessary, I vacuum the house three times a week because that's what my husband expects.
- I spent an hour on the phone listening to a girlfriend talk about her marital problems when I needed, instead, to be helping my children get ready for bed.
- I have an acquaintance who thinks of me as her best friend, so she calls me constantly. She's unaware that I'm terribly turned off by her, but I can't muster the courage to talk with her about it.
- I volunteered for nursery duty last Sunday at church even though I didn't want to do so because I had just volunteered the week before.
- I didn't say a word when my dad criticized my parenting decisions, even though he had completely miscalculated what had happened.

On and on the list went as Anita recounted the many instances in which she set aside her own legitimate needs in order to make someone else happy or to keep them appeased. As she completed the reading of her list, I heaved a great sigh and remarked, "Wow! All that effort to satisfy everyone else must be emotionally draining! No wonder depression and frustration visit you so easily. You're wearing yourself out."

How about you? Can you relate to Anita's plight? Do you ever find yourself going into a mode of self-deferral to the extent that you feel others are taking advantage of your good nature? If so, you may be in a pattern of unhealthy people pleasing.

As we tackle this subject, let's first put the issue of people pleasing into proper perspective by asking: Is it wrong for you to attempt to be pleasing? The answer, of course, is no. Not only is people pleasing not a bad characteristic; it is also good and necessary if families and organizations are going to grow and thrive. Our world leans too much in the direction of self-absorption and insensitivity, so it is wonderfully refreshing to find persons who take it upon themselves to be an uplifting, tuned-in presence in others' lives. The Bible, in fact, teaches that service is a cornerstone trait for the followers of Christ. "With humility of mind," says Philippians 2:3, "let each of you regard one another as more important than himself." In John 12:26, Jesus stated even more strongly, "If anyone serves Me, . . . the Father will honor him." Clearly, kindness or self-sacrifice has its place in a Christian's life choices.

As you might imagine, though, it is possible to carry a good characteristic too far to the extent that it actually feeds unhealthy emotions or relational habits. In Anita's case, she had committed her entire life to being friendly, available, or flexible; yet, the overuse of those traits directly contributed to depression and a simmering anger. As the years had passed and the number of frustrating incidents piled up, she had found herself less and less effective in her primary relationships. To put it in her own words, "I'm getting to the point where I dread talking to anyone because I don't know what they're going to ask of me next."

Unhealthy people pleasing can be defined as the tendency to cater to others' preferences to the detriment of personal well-being. Contrary to the Christian idea of serving others unselfishly, it helps perpetuate patterns that can be manipulative or, at the very least, insensitive.

In one session, Anita told me, "From the days of my youth, I've been trained to believe in the virtues of kindness, forgiveness, and tolerance. I still believe in those traits, but I guess I'm having to learn the other side of the equation. No one ever talked with me about how I'm supposed to respond when people are rude, manipulative, or self-centered. Looks like I'm going to have to toughen up so I don't feel used."

"I agree with you about the toughening-up part," I replied, "although we both would agree that our goal is not going to be to make you over into a mean-as-the-devil tyrant who won't take any trash off of anyone." We both chuckled as we realized that would never happen anyway.

As you too consider making the necessary adjustments to bring your people pleasing into balance, first recognize that awareness will be a very necessary ingredient in the change process. You will need to take a full inventory of yourself, as Anita did, to determine just how extensive this pattern is in your life.

To put that awareness process in motion, look over the following statements common to people pleasers and check the ones that often would apply to you:

_____ 1. I have opinions about right and wrong, yet I will not always stand firm when faced with a persuasive person.

_____ 2. I can be motivated by guilt.

_____ 3. It really bothers me if I have upset someone.

_____ 4. I feel that I try harder to make relationships work than others do.

_____ 5. People would be surprised to know about the resentment that is bottled up inside me.

_____ 6. When another person is angry, I go into the appeaser mode.

_____ 7. If my decisions are called into question, I feel I'd better have a good justification.

_____ 8. When I do something for my own pleasure, I may feel selfish.

_____ 9. Too often, I'll do someone else's chores because they won't do them.

_____ 10. Sometimes I just try too hard to be nice.

_____ 11. I have to tread lightly due to key people who are moody.

_____ 12. It seems as though my world is full of requirements and duties.

_____   13. With certain people, I find myself measuring my words very carefully.

_____   14. Even when I am nice to others, it seems that they still want more.

_____   15. There are times when I just give up on being taken seriously or feeling understood.

_____   16. I can let people determine too much of my schedule or priorities.

_____   17. Too often, I explain my reasoning over and over, even though it is clear that the other person won't hear what I have to say.

_____   18. I have stayed in bad relationships long after I knew they were not good for me.

_____   19. Being firm can be hard for me at times.

_____   20. It seems that others will accept me only as long as I conform to their ways.

Most of us have had circumstances where we bent too far in the direction of other peoples' whims or demands. However, if you find yourself doing this too frequently, it is an indicator that your people pleasing is likely to be your own downfall. If you responded to five or fewer of the above statements, your people pleasing is probably not a dominant trait. In fact, you may lean more in the direction of a headstrong pattern. If you responded to six to nine of the statements, you may have moments when your people pleasing produces some compromising tendencies, but you would also be expected to balance that tendency with proper assertiveness. If you responded to ten or more of the statements, you are likely to have frequent moments when you are too accommodating for your own good. There is a strong likelihood that you set aside your own good preferences for the sake of keeping others off your back . . . and it is also likely that those efforts do not produce rewarding results.

The Requirements of People Pleasing

What is it about people pleasing that ultimately contributes to emotional and relational discord? Let's examine four self-imposed "requirements" that often accompany this pattern.

The Requirement to Be Responsible for What Is Not Yours

A central component in healthy, thriving relationships is the willingness of each individual to be responsible for personal issues. For instance, if a man has a problem with his temper, it is his job to say, "I know this is wrong, and I need to learn about myself in such a way that will help me correct my inappropriateness." If a woman falls too easily into behaviors of insecurity, it is her job to examine the thinking patterns that are bringing her down. In these circumstances, it would be wrong to assume that others must behave correctly before that temper or that insecurity can be remedied. Whereas we are each somewhat dependent upon our circumstances to bring us some measure of satisfaction, we each also have the capability to rise above difficult circumstances to chart a course toward full and productive patterns.

People pleasers, however, tend to overlook the reality that others are responsible for their own problems. They tell themselves, "I must be the one to keep other people feeling good." Whether through others' manipulation or their own false guilt, they step into the role of caretaker when they ultimately do not belong there.

Anita, for instance, told me, "Ted likes spending time with our two daughters, but sometimes I worry that they are going to be rambunctious and set him off. You know how kids can be!"

"So what do you do when you sense your girls are becoming agitated around your husband?"

"*Panic* may be too strong of a word, but my anxiety definitely goes way up. I know he gets too cranky sometimes, so I often will redirect the girls onto something else, or I may take one or both of them with me to run an errand."

"Would you say this contributes to some of the burnout you often experience?"

"Oh, definitely! I constantly feel like it's my job to keep the peace, but it wears me out sometimes because it's so hard to stay a step ahead of a nine-year-old and a five-year-old."

Do you see the error in Anita's family interaction? She knows her husband has a temper, so quite naturally she would prefer to be free from its ill effects. Yet she is overlooking an undeniable truth: She cannot always monitor Ted's moods! That's his job. While there may be moments when she could be a soothing presence, there are also moments when she can't run interference. She can't always direct Ted's moods or the girls' reactions to him.

Somewhere along the way (usually early in life) people pleasers have picked up the erroneous notion that they must assume responsibility for other persons' moods. Do you remember Anita's description of her early years with her father? She had assumed that she should be very calculating around him so she would not upset or displease him. Though she was not directly told that she was responsible for his mood, that is the assumption she made . . . and in her adult years, she generalized that thought by taking responsibility for the moods of anyone close to her.

How about you? Do you find yourself taking responsibility for others' moods or behaviors even when it is probable that you won't be allowed to succeed in that task? While it is good and desirable for you to be attentive to the way your choices affect others, you have crossed the line of healthiness when you make yourself primarily responsible for others' actions.

The Requirement of Enablement

When people pleasers assume unnecessary responsibility for others, it sets into motion the possibility of an even deeper problem—enabling others in their unhealthy ways.

In an ideal world, you would expect that your acts of kindness or your attempts to be sensitive would not only be met with appreciation, but they would be reciprocated in fair measure. Ideally you could think, "I'll treat you nice with the calm assurance that you will do the same in reverse."

This is no ideal world! People can be unappreciative, lazy, unwilling to compromise, and manipulative. Therefore, when you act in pleasing ways, there is a possibility that others will think, "This is an excellent opportunity for me to indulge my selfish desires." Not every person is this way, but enough are that it warrants caution when you choose to serve others. Only naive persons assume that their pleasing behavior will be universally met with right responses.

When people pleasers go too far in their pleasant ways, they may inadvertently be guilty of encouraging others to continue in selfish or disrespectful behavior. Instead of receiving kind gestures with a spirit of gratitude, some people respond with an attitude of deservedness. In the midst of their selfishness, they may think, "I expect you to continue treating me special . . . and don't even think that I'm supposed to let go of my rude behavior." As you continue to play the appeaser role, you then help that person sustain behavior that is clearly wrong. This is called enablement.

For instance, Anita told me of an incident when her husband left her at home sweating over heavy yard work while he went to a sports bar to watch a ball game. They had specifically agreed to finishing the project together before going on to other activities. "But you have to understand Ted. He does this stuff to me constantly. He may initially agree to help with a chore, but before you know it, I wind up doing it all!"

"Why do you suppose he does this?" I asked.

Her answer was the classic response of an enabler, "Because he knows I'll do it." It never dawned on Anita to save the chore for him to complete later. "I'll take care of it myself" was her motto, and Ted was milking it for all he could.

Do you ever find yourself in the enabler role? At work, do people know you will cover for their ineptitudes? In marriage, does your spouse pull back from being a full partner because you can handle it all? Do your kids have poor housekeeping habits because they know you'll pick up after them? Do friends dodge distasteful tasks because they know you will do them instead? If so, your people pleasing may actually be *irresponsible* on your part since it ultimately keeps their bad habits and attitudes in motion.

The Requirement to Deny What Is Healthy

I have spoken with parents of teenagers who will say, "I'd rather let my son and his friends have their beer parties here at home than have them doing it behind my back where it is far less safe." I have heard employees say, "I know that I take on more work than I'm required, but I want to be sure that we stay in business, so I've got to do it." I have heard people say of their friends, "Maybe I don't agree with her lifestyle choices, but she needs me to be there for her, so sometimes you've just got to compromise for the future of the relationship."

In each of these scenarios, the people pleasers are presumably being nice because they have higher goals to achieve. In many instances, though, they are openly abetting others' unhealthy choices because they are afraid of others' reactions if they choose to do what is best. Being able to point to their own cooperative or "helpful" behavior, these people pleasers can fool themselves into sidestepping the difficult choices that often come alongside firm values.

As an example, Anita told me how she was frustrated with her parents' insistence that they must always celebrate her children's birthdays at their home. "Ted's family lives fairly near, but they are always given the leftover times with my kids. I know they don't like it, and I'd really like to accommodate them. I don't want to hassle with my parents' anger, so we just go along with my parents to avoid the fuss."

Was Anita's management of this dilemma good? Not really. It would be fair for her to tell her parents that she wanted the other set of grandparents to have special times with the kids too. As a daughter-in-law, it would be healthy for her to be fair-minded in the way she juggled the needs of all the extended family, but in her efforts to please her parents, she felt required to deny the healthiness of such fair-mindedness, choosing instead to adhere blindly to a lopsided way of thinking.

It may be troubling to admit it, but other people may be unable or unwilling to recognize the unhealthiness in their preferences. For example, the teens who want to get drunk or the employers who take advantage of their employees or the friends who choose poor values may each have their rationale for doing what they do. Yet despite their rationale, they can still be wrong! People pleasers can mistakenly assume that they have to keep peace with these folks, so they often blindly overlook others' unhealthy priorities for the sake of getting along.

The Requirement of Disrespect Toward Oneself

Suppose you talk with me about something heavy on your heart. You pour your emotions out hoping to receive some friendly encouragement; instead, I reply, "Why don't you just face the reality that your feelings and perspectives don't matter." How would you feel?

If I spoke in an openly insulting manner, you would be deeply offended. You would cry foul, and you would probably determine not to be open with me again.

No one likes to be insulted or belittled by outsiders; yet despite their normal desire for respect, people pleasers often find themselves in a position of being disrespected. What is most absurd is that the person showing the most disrespect to them is self!

Think back on some of the instances Anita described. She let her parents act in overbearing ways toward her. Her husband did not factor in her needs when setting up his schedule. Her kids could easily figure out how to sidestep her principles. What was her reaction? She would go along with it! It is clear that these key people showed low regard at times for her value, but the real tragedy lay in the fact that Anita did not respect herself either. Though she may not have verbalized it, her behavior indicated that she did not hold her own decisions or beliefs in high regard.

Has this ever happened to you? You may realize that others do not factor in your needs as they interact with you, but are you aware that your overcompliance may indicate that you too agree with this low assessment of you?

As we consider the goal of bringing people-pleasing behavior into balance, let's affirm that we do not need to go to the other extreme of being completely self-absorbed or blatantly insensitive to others' needs. That would be too strong of a pendulum swing, but let's affirm that we do want to pursue interpersonal behaviors that uphold human dignity . . . toward other people in our lives and toward ourselves.

I spoke with Anita about finding balance in her key relationships. "I deeply respect your desire to be a cooperative and uplifting presence in the lives of those closest to you. We need more people in our world like you who are conscientious about how their behavior can impact someone else's quality of life. My concern, as I listen to your story, is that you have taken a good trait too far. Unfortunately, you can encounter some people who are willing to respond to your good nature by using you for their own selfish gain, and that's not good. In fact, let's take the thought one step further by saying that there can be instances when your people pleasing is an act of irresponsibility."

That last statement startled her. "Irresponsible? I could think of a lot of words to describe me, but that would not have been one of them." She sat for a moment in silent reflection then said, "But I happen to agree that you're right. For several years, I've been having this nagging discomfort as I felt that something wasn't right in my life."

"Anita, when you experience emotions like depression or anxiety or lingering frustration, that can be your mind's way of saying that something is not right within yourself. Those emotions can be signals indicating that you need some new directions."

"That's an interesting way to look at it," she replied. Shaking her head cautiously, she said, "Boy, I've got some changing to do. I can see where I need to be different, but it's going to require a monumental effort, and a shock to others' systems, if I am going to reverse some of my patterns."

"I am basing my thoughts on the notion that you can't really afford to go on in a lifestyle that ultimately is so disrespectful toward yourself. In the name of being kind to others, you are letting yourself be treated, at times, with indignity. If that continues, the emotional garbage is going to build so powerfully inside that eventually you will be no good to anyone."

Can you relate? As you continue in the book, it is my desire that you maintain your loving and giving nature but that you do it in a responsible fashion. Sometimes the most loving behavior is not comfortable. Sometimes loving behavior requires limits, and it may cause others to feel frustrated with you. Can you handle that?

The good news is this: When you learn to maintain solid boundaries, and as you gain balance between pleasing behavior and assertiveness, get ready for some major improvements in your relationships. You can expect to have a cleaner emotional system yourself, which can translate into more rewarding relationships.

To bring balance to your people pleasing, I will be walking you through four areas. In the book's first section, we will develop a keen awareness of the factors that are a part of excessive people pleasing, and how the negative effects of people pleasing will play out in your emotions. Next, we will examine how your people pleasing developed. We will examine some of the early teachings and experiences common to people with this pattern for the purpose of identifying alternatives to your old habits. In the third section, we will look more intently at the traits needed to keep you from going too far in your pleasing behavior. We will explore, for instance, how to get away from a mindset of duty, developing instead an approach toward life grounded in freedom. Also, we will affirm the necessity of boundaries and firmness and assertiveness. Then finally, we will look at ways to apply your balanced thinking to common settings . . . with your mate, your children, and your coworkers.

As Anita counseled with me, she smiled as she said, "I had no idea that my pleasing behavior could be tied to so many issues. Looks like I've got some waking up to do."

Would you be able to echo Anita's response? Armed with awareness of healthy and safe patterns of emotional management, you too can expect to find optimism instead of carrying burdens that do not belong on your shoulders.

For Personal Reflection

What pleasing aspects of your life are truly good?

_____

_____

_____

When does your people-pleasing behavior cross the line, ultimately bringing tension and frustration into your life?

_____

_____

_____

_____

_____

What would you say is the difference between healthy and unhealthy people pleasing?

_____

_____

_____

_____

Look back over the twenty-point checklist in this chapter. Which two or three statements most accurately describe your problems with unhealthy people pleasing?

_____

_____

_____

_____

In what circumstances do you take on the responsibilities that others should take upon themselves?

_____

_____

_____

_____

In what way is your people pleasing linked to feelings of disrespect toward yourself?

_____

_____

_____

_____

In the days to come, how might you begin to reverse the trend of unhealthy people pleasing?

_____

_____

_____

_____

Chapter 2

Seven Identifiers of People Pleasers

As Tommy walked into my office, I thought to myself that he had one of the most engaging smiles I had seen in some time. In his early forties, he was dressed casually with khakis and sneakers, causing me to guess that he worked for one of the large companies nearby that specialized in some sort of computer products. (These guys always seemed to dress more comfortably than, say, an insurance salesman.) Sure enough, I learned that he was a product development specialist for a large company just a couple of miles away from my office that sold computer components to the telecommunications industry.

When I asked him to tell me his reason for being in my office, with the same engaging smile he said, "Oh, I've been having problems with depression for at least two or three years, and I can't seem to shake it." I didn't comment on the inconsistency between his words and his facial features, but I made a mental note of it. Tommy went on to tell me that he was chronically overworked, which then caused tension at home with his wife, Nicole. She regularly complained that she had her hands full working as a second-grade teacher while also trying to keep up with their two teenage sons.

"Nicole is the sweetest lady I know," he explained, although something told me that he didn't always think she was sweet. "She's got a good point when she says I should try to get home at better hours. She points out that my coworkers don't stay as late as I do; so, she knows I could do something about it."

"Well, could you?"

"Yeah, I guess so, but that's easier said than done. I don't mean to brag, but everyone at the office knows that I can unclog log jams better than just about anyone else, so I'm constantly getting calls to help others out. What really chaps off Nicole is when I agree to go in to work on weekends. She tells me I should say no, but I tell her it's not that easy."

"So, where does the depression fit in?"

"I get real discouraged because I feel that no matter what decision I make, someone's going to be mad at me. If I do what my wife wants, my peers at work are ticked. If I try to do the job I feel I'm paid to do, my wife is upset. Then there's the rest of my family. If I try to spend time with my brother, my in-laws say I ignore them. If I miss one of my sons' after-school activities, they mope around and act hurt. If we decide not to spend a holiday with my parents, they're mad for weeks."

Amazingly, he was still smiling as he relayed these thoughts.

Tommy's presenting problem was depression, but as in the case with Anita, he was never going to be free from his emotional strains until he came to terms with his pervasive tendency to please others, even when it ultimately harmed his own quality of life.

Seven Signs of People Pleasers

When I work with people like Tommy or Anita, one of my initial goals is to help them recognize the signs that they are feeding a pattern of living that will bring harm to them. In many cases the telltale signs are very obvious; yet to the person with the problem, they are so common that they recur with hardly any forethought or conscious planning. By making people pleasers aware of the components to this pattern, I hope to raise their realization that they can choose to continue in these tendencies or they can choose to pursue healthier alternatives.

The Seven Identifiers of People Pleasers

1. Duty as a driving motivator
2. Legitimate needs quickly set aside
3. Equating decisiveness with hurting others
4. Difficulty living within limits
5. Sensitivity to judgments
6. The need to keep life controlled
7. Dishonesty about who you really are

Sign #1: Duty as a Driving Motivator

Whether the organization is a family, a church, a place of business, or a social structure, each person brings differing skills and abilities to the table that can potentially benefit the group. A successful organization is one where the role of each member is clearly defined and implemented. When people's lives are as intricately woven together as they are in any organization, it stands to reason that all individuals will be required to pull their own weight in one form or another.

Think about the various roles you play in any given week . . . parent, sibling, spouse, engineer, salesperson, friend, or mentor. Each role carries with it its own set of expectations and requirements. Whether you are consciously aware of it or not, you have a set of attitudes and behaviors that others assume you will fulfill.

As you approach your roles, you have two options regarding the mindset that will accompany your behavior: (1) You can willfully choose to do what you do because that is your genuine preference, or (2) you can live up to your role's expectations because you feel compelled to do so.

People pleasers tend to operate with choice #2 leading the way, even though they may try to convince themselves they are really opting for #1. Duty and compulsion often outweigh free choice in their decision making. On the surface, hardly anyone else may know just how strong the sense of duty is, but behind the scenes, it is powerfully evident.

To get an idea of the role of duty in your motivation, ask yourself:

- Is there ever a time when I quietly tell myself that I shouldn't have let someone else persuade me to do what I really didn't want to do?
- Do I take on more commitments or responsibility than my schedule really allows?
- Do I do what I do for fear that others might not do it at all?
- Are my decisions influenced by the fear of disappointing someone if I told them no?
- Once in the midst of a project, do I ever think about all the other things I should be doing instead?
- Do I frequently wish I was doing something other than what I am doing?

Usually people pleasers have such strong notions about what *should* be done or how things are *supposed* to unfold that they feel they have no other option but to proceed, even when they have an intuitive sense that they need to be expending their energies elsewhere. It's as though they think, "If something's wrong or if someone is in need, it's my job to take care of it."

As I got to know Tommy through our counseling sessions, I learned that he was not the only one in his family with people-pleasing tendencies. His father had owned a local auto mechanic shop when Tommy was a boy, so naturally, he spent many days in his youth working alongside his dad. Looking back, he told me, "My dad was the kind of guy who never had an unpleasant word to say about anybody. He was really friendly and would always take time out to shoot the breeze with anyone who came along."

"Sounds like he was a good guy who made friends easily."

"Well, yeah, I guess you could say he was a good guy, but sometimes it wasn't always so."

I raised my eyebrows as I encouraged Tommy to continue his story.

"Dad had this deep conviction that he should never do anything to disappoint people; so he was constantly making promises that would eventually put him into a bind. For example, if someone needed a new clutch and they told him they had to leave town that afternoon, he'd put everything aside to get the job done; but he'd get so far behind on his other jobs that he'd have to work late into the night to keep the rest of the customers off his back."

"Did he ever complain about the deadlines others would impose on him?"

"All the time! I guess he lectured me at least five hundred times about how he was in the service industry, which meant that it was his obligation to keep paying customers happy. He was duty-bound to do whatever had to be done even if his life was miserable as a result." Of course, that was a mindset that became emblazoned in Tommy's mind.

Is it good for people to honor their responsibilities in a dutiful manner? Yes . . . up to a point. Responsibility is best pursued when the mind is motivated by free will. While some responsible acts are indeed a drudgery (cleaning bathrooms or filing expense reports), people are at their best when they *choose* to act right as opposed to doing so because of sheer obligation. As an example, Tommy needed to realize that his father's emphasis on helping others was good *as long as* he was allowed to say no when the request proved to be unfeasible at the time.

If people pleasers are to ease their emotional tensions, they will need to evaluate their many tasks by asking, "Is this something I would choose if I lived as a truly free person?"

Sign #2: Legitimate Needs Quickly Set Aside

No person is completely self-sufficient. From the very first day of life, we count on others to know our needs and help us find satisfaction by addressing matters essential to personal well-being.

Think of the things that are needed in your life as you pursue contentment and success. You need love, cooperation, connection, and encouragement. You need to have matters of survival addressed—money, food, shelter, and clothing. You need emotional nourishment found through experiences of personal confiding, laughter, and crying on a caring shoulder. These things, and many more, are necessary for you to develop the sense that your life is heading in a purposeful direction, that you count for something.

People pleasers recognize that needs are a natural part of life, that there is a necessary interdependence that we all require. Their focus regarding those needs, however, tends to be lopsided in that they readily acknowledge others' needs while regularly denying the real nature of their own.

Let's go back to Anita, the woman who wanted to learn how to appease her husband's and father's anger. She could cite numerous examples of times when she would respond to one of their needs while simultaneously discounting her own. For instance, if Ted wanted to do some work in the garage without being bothered by one of their kids, Anita would take upon herself the task of running interference. "Don't go out there and bother Daddy," she would say to the girls. She had no assurance that he would ever arrange his schedule to accommodate the activities she had planned, nor did he show any concern that Anita was thrust in the role of the enforcer while he enjoyed uninterrupted peace away from family conflict.

"That kind of thing happens all the time," she would complain.

"Do you ever say anything to him about it?"

"Oh, I used to," she said with a sigh of defeat, "but my words mostly fell on deaf ears."

Through the course of our sessions, Anita and I discussed how she could address her own legitimate needs in three ways: (1) She could give herself permission to say no when someone else's request interfered with her own legitimate and immediate needs; (2) she could more firmly coach others in the ways they could respond more appropriately to those needs; (3) even in instances when others were not attuned to her, she could still act on her own behalf to take initiatives that would at least partially satisfy her needs.

For instance, one Saturday Anita needed to run some quick errands without being encumbered by the girls. She knew Ted was available to watch them, though he'd probably feel that the girls might interfere with the football game on TV. Whereas she would normally defer to Ted's preferences, I coached her to realize that it was OK to ask him to help her in this instance.

The assertive thinking that accompanied this new way of acting was quite unnatural to her. "It feels like I'm being selfish," she explained. Like so many other people pleasers, Anita had not yet distinguished the difference between selfishness and legitimate self-preservation.

Sign #3: Equating Decisiveness with Hurting Others

In one of our discussions, Tommy told me that he had tried on a couple of occasions to tell his mother that he could not arrange his schedule to meet her preferences for holiday gatherings. "She wanted all the family to be together on Memorial Day; but we had already committed to spend that day with some friends that we hadn't seen in some time. When I explained the situation to my mom she said it was OK, but her tone of voice told me a very different story. She was crushed and I knew it."

"So when you know she's upset, how does that leave you feeling?"

"Well, I feel awful! I hate it when my decisions cause someone else to grieve like that."

Did Tommy's decision cause his mother to hurt? Well, yes and no. Yes, she honestly felt disappointed and hurt because he chose to spend time with friends (by the way, his decision was a real departure from the norm because he had virtually always spent any holiday with her rather than with friends). Was the hurt caused by Tommy's mean spirit or by his mother's own mindset of deservedness?

In this instance, the mother's hurt could be attributed to her own selfish insistence that her son had to cater to her in the manner she decreed. Tommy explained that she had always been very demanding regarding his schedule, and she left little room for him to have separate priorities. So even though she indeed felt hurt, it would not be accurate to say that Tommy caused it. She brought it on herself with her own self-preoccupation.

People pleasers often assume more responsibility for others' emotional reactions than is really warranted. With an overdeveloped conscience, they can falsely assume that if they make a decision which results in another person's feeling angry or disappointed or frustrated, they must then take it upon themselves to relieve that person's struggle.

Consider how easily this pattern can play out:

- A mother puts a restriction on a child, resulting in fussing and fuming. The parent then wonders, *Am I being too hard on the kid?*

- A wife decides not to go to her husband's company dinner because she is offended by his overindulgent use of alcohol. He won't speak to her for days, leaving her questioning, "Does this mean I'm being disloyal?"

- After a man tells his friend that he cannot support the friend's charity in the fashion he would like, the friend is clearly offended. The man thinks, *Maybe I ought to write him a check just to get him off my back.*

- A woman's supervisor puts a pile of work on her desk, giving her an impossible deadline to complete it. When she tells the supervisor that something is going to be left undone so she can do the new task in the allotted time, the supervisor walks away in a huff. The worker is left wondering if she's just not efficient enough.

In each of these examples, a person's decisiveness drew a frustrated response from the other individual involved. Unnecessarily, the people pleasers assumed that they caused that person's emotional distress, not considering that the distress was caused instead by ingredients within that other person's personality outside the people pleaser's control.

Sign #4: Difficulty Living Within Limits

Every one of us is limited in what we can accomplish. Time, of course, causes us to be limited regarding the number of projects we can manage in any given day. Likewise, we each have finite capabilities, meaning there are just some things we do not have the skills to do. Also, we have a limited capacity to enter another person's mind, introducing influential thoughts. We simply cannot *make* others think as we would like.

That stated, many people pleasers attempt to live as if they do not have the same limits on their lives as others do. They will push themselves to be all that others expect—and more. Internally, they are driven by the requirement to be more than what they are capable of being.

Think, for example, about some of the expectations others may have for you that are inconsistent with your personal limits. For instance:

- Your spouse may expect you to read his or her mood even though you are limited in knowing exactly how to interpret every behavior.
- Friends may expect you to alter your schedule despite your inability to be "all things to all people."
- Coworkers may expect you to solve their problems, ignoring the fact that you are limited in the things that you can give your attention to.
- Extended family members may assume that you should have the same priorities they have, not allowing you the leeway to factor in the separate needs of your spouse's family.

Recall that Tommy had a reputation at work for being the ultimate problem solver. He truly possessed not only a superior IQ but also an uncanny common sense that enabled him to logically break down difficult circumstances in ways others could not. Tommy's problem then was not in his intellectual functioning but in his emotional reactions to the many people who pressed him to solve their problems for them.

Let's affirm that it was a good thing for Tommy to be helpful to others. We all have moments when we need to turn to an expert who can streamline difficult circumstances, and Tommy was one of the best in the telecommunications business. In taking on the problems that others brought to him, though, Tommy failed frequently to acknowledge his limits. He failed to explain that when he took time to solve one problem, the original task he was supposed to be solving was left undone. He could not do two things at once. As a result, Tommy suffered from bouts of anger and tension because he constantly seemed to have more on his plate than he could handle.

As you examine your own life, what limits do you see in yourself? You probably recognize in many ways just how finite you are. You cannot be all things to all people. Now consider another question: Who in your world would like you to ignore the truth about your limits as they attempt to push you to feel or think or behave in ways that are unreasonable? If you are like Tommy, you may have many people who want to overlook your limitations.

He once explained to me, "It's like people want me to be Superman, but I'm not! I'd like to just be able to say 'Back off; I can't do it all.'"

"Then why not say just that?" I replied.

Tommy grinned for a moment, then said, "Why did I know you'd respond that way?" He shook his head and continued, "It's just so unnatural for me to tell someone that I can't do something. It would feel so awkward."

"I suspect the awkwardness stems from the admission that you are not only limited in the number of things you can accomplish, but also in your ability to control how others feel about you. Keep this in mind: Others won't acknowledge your limits until you first demonstrate that you acknowledge your own limits. In a sense, you may have to train people to think a little less loftily about your capabilities."

When you fail to live within limits, your body has a way of forcing you to recognize them anyway. This is often why people experience heart attacks, high blood pressure, ulcers, depression, anxiety, and the like. You have a choice to set your limits on your own good terms or have your body set limits through a more severe measure.

Sign #5: Sensitivity to Judgments

Do you recall the first time you were judged? You were undoubtedly so young that you cannot actually remember it. From the very earliest years, toddlers hear comments like, "That was excellent!" "Young man, why did you do that? You know better!" "Good girl!" "That was great; now let's see if you can do it again." "What in the world is wrong with you?"

These, and many similar statements, imply some form of judgment. Do they sound familiar? As you matured from childhood into adulthood, you continued receiving judgments on a wide array of subjects: your achievements, your looks, your social skills, your emotional expressions, your priorities, your failures, and your communication skills. Despite biblical admonitions that humans are not to be in the business of judging other humans, we do it every day.

It would have been nice if we'd been taught how to keep the judgments of others in their proper perspective. In the best sense, others' pronouncements can let you know how you are perceived, and they can be a useful guide to steer you through the intricacies required to adjust your personality with those around you. In the worst sense, though, the judgments of others can cause you to lose confidence or to stray from the path of healthy choices as you seek favor from potential critics.

Remember how Anita tended to cower and suppress her emotions when faced with the possibility of receiving her husband's or father's anger? These two men tended to rush to judgment regarding her decisions. "I hardly ever get praised when I do something right, but boy are they quick to pounce when I do something wrong," she told me. "Somehow they have each taken it upon themselves to be both judge and jury regarding the decisions I make in my life."

"What effect does this critical or judgmental spirit have on you?"

"Well, internally I'm thinking that these are two dunder-headed egomaniacs who have no business passing judgment on me; but as far as my behavior goes . . . well, let's just say that I'll do almost anything to keep them off my back."

The problem with Anita's decision was that not only did it not solve her tensions, but it increased them. As she showed she was intimidated by the possibility of their judgment, they continued all the more. What is worse, she had begun judging herself just as harshly as they would. For instance, she once told me how she felt guilty for accepting an invitation to a "girl's night out" dinner with a few of her closest friends. "My dad always made sure my mom knew that her first priority was him. That's the kind of influence I grew up with. Even though Ted isn't quite as blatantly chauvinistic, he doesn't take well to my being too independent. He says that too much of that stuff is bad and that I'd better not get too used to going out away from him."

"Were you doing anything immoral or irresponsible by going out with your friends?"

"Heavens no! We're the tamest bunch of gals you could meet. Yet, the whole time I was out that night, I had this nagging sense that I was doing something wrong. I couldn't enjoy myself because I just knew I was out of line."

Have you ever had a similar experience of being so keenly aware of others' judgments that you could not let yourself be you? Perhaps, like Anita, you have become so conscious of others' pronouncements that you take them too seriously. Be willing to hear what others say about your decisions, but also sidestep the misguided notion that these people have the prerogative to declare if you are a good or bad person because of those decisions. No human is effective in playing the role of God.

Sign #6: The Need to Keep Life Controlled

Not all people-pleasing behavior is motivated by fear or guilt. People pleasers are not always manipulated to do what they do. Sometimes your people-pleasing behavior has a self-serving aspect to it linked to the desire to be in control.

Tommy, for example, could readily bemoan the fact that other people easily took advantage of his good nature because he was very handy in so many ways. During one of our conversations he admitted, "Sometimes I do things for other people because of a more self-oriented reasoning."

I did not know where he was going with that statement; so I cocked my head and replied, "What are you getting at?"

"Well, it's simple. In certain areas, the lack of order drives me crazy. When people in my world do a sloppy job, I figure that somewhere down the road I'll probably be negatively affected. When I step in to save the day, sometimes it's because I'm letting people manipulate me, but sometimes it's because I want things in order and doing it myself may be the best way to get what I want."

I had to hand it to Tommy; at least he was honest!

Many people pleasers, like Tommy, operate as they do because they do not like the prospect of having loose ends in their world. Frustrated that those loose ends will end up hurting them, they may act in ways that appear to be helpful to others when in fact they are primarily thinking of their own needs. Can you spot the self-serving, controlling behavior in the following examples?

- An overly helpful mom constantly picks up after the rest of the family as opposed to taking the time to give them the instructions to learn how to do things for themselves.
- An employee goes out of her way to be helpful, then refers to those helpful incidences during her employee review with her supervisor.
- A son-in-law "jumps through the hoops" that his in-laws lay out, knowing he will later be able to persuade his wife to do what he wants.
- A husband does extra chores around the house so his wife can have no "ammunition" against him when she discovers the mistakes he has made.

Many instances of people pleasing can actually be recognized as an attempt to keep life under control. So let's ponder for a moment: Is it always wrong to want control? When persons are merely attempting to maintain reasonable order or structure, it is not wrong to seek some control. When people are devious, when they harbor ulterior motives, or when they seek to manipulate others against their will, then yes, it can be wrong to attempt to control.

On the surface, most people pleasers appear to be sufficiently self-effacing not to warrant suspicions of manipulative behavior. But don't be fooled! In some cases, people pleasing is part of a larger plan to put others into a subservient position.

Sign #7: Dishonesty About Who You Really Are

Though the vast majority of people pleasers would not be described as liars, there is a persistent feature in their life patterns that can be unflattering to admit. They are frequently dishonest about their real feelings or perceptions. While not openly telling falsehoods, they are allowing others to draw false conclusions. For instance, consider the people pleaser who is asked to help on a project that he has no interest in and no time to give to it. When he says, "Sure, I'll be glad to help," how honest is that? Through the smile on his face and through his helpful acts, he is openly encouraging others to assume that he feels something he does not.

"Gee, now that you put it to me like that," Anita told me, "my people-pleasing behavior doesn't sound quite so honorable."

"I don't mean to put more guilt on you," I countered, "since you already operate with more than your fair share of that. I want you to be motivated to take a hard look at what the healthy life entails and aim for that."

Dishonesty is not part of a healthy lifestyle. In growing, thriving relationships, traits like openness and full disclosure are present in large doses. With a wide variety of personal needs and priorities, it is highly predictable that in any relationship differences will emerge often. Healthy relationships not only allow for these differences to surface; they *want* them to surface.

I explained to Anita, "If I were your husband or father, I would want you to talk freely with me about the things you feel differently about. Maybe I wouldn't always like what you tell me, but I'd still want you to feel that you could be honest with me."

Wide-eyed, she responded, "Wow! That's actually the way you think? How refreshing! I don't really sense that anyone close to me really wants me to be that honest. Whenever I get real about my needs, I just get invalidations or criticisms."

"Then what you have is not closeness at all. People don't really know you as well as they may think they do."

That last thought is often very sobering to people pleasers. One of the most common frustrations they experience is emotional isolation, often due to the fact that they can't, or won't, let people know who they really are. The possibility of ridicule or rejection or judgment keeps them in an oppressed mode; then their dishonest behavior assures emptiness.

Do you want a healthy way of life with relationships that are based upon respect and acceptance and authenticity? If so, you may need to take a hard look at the seven signs of people pleasing as you begin evaluating how you may inadvertently be contributing to your own frustration.

People such as Tommy and Anita have concluded that they can ill afford to continue with the emotional strains brought on by the dysfunctions in their primary relationships. They decided that adjustments are needed, beginning with Self, if they are ever going to participate in productive relating patterns.

Remember, though, that some people may *want* you to continue in your old imbalanced people-pleasing style, so they may offer resistance. Be prepared. In the chapters to follow, we will explore how to break your people-pleasing pattern without also having to lose the good parts of your pleasing personality.

For Personal Reflection

What duties do you feel bound to keep that are not really essential?

_____

_____

_____

As you act helpfully toward others, what personal needs of yours may go lacking?

_____

_____

_____

Think of a time when your decisiveness prompted another person to feel hurt or let down. At such a moment, how can you determine if that person's frustration was really caused by you or by his or her demanding nature?

_____

_____

_____

Which of your legitimate limits do others seem to want you to ignore?

_____

_____

_____

_____

When you sense someone is judgmental toward you, how does this affect your emotions? How does it affect your people-pleasing tendencies?

_____

_____

_____

_____

In what ways do you over-attempt to be in control?

_____

_____

_____

_____

As you are in your people-pleasing mode, in what ways might you project an image that is not really consistent with what you truly feel inwardly?

_____

_____

_____

_____

Chapter 3

Making Emotional Exchanges

Surely you have been in a situation requiring you to go to the store and exchange an item. Suppose, for example, your mother gives you a sweater for Christmas that is entirely the wrong size. You'll say, "Though I'm pleased that Mother wanted me to have this sweater, I'll have to take it back and trade it for one that fits. Then I can get some use out of it." Not only would that be a normal thing to do; it's something we've all done at one time or another.

People pleasers are in a position of making exchanges, only we're not talking about exchanging tangible items, but emotional responses. Over the course of time, in their personal development, these people have picked up emotional habits that do not fit. Many carry unnecessary guilt and fear and anxiety. Through repetitive experiences they have learned to claim ownership for emotions that they need not own. As they enter the adult years they can even tell themselves that they probably ought not to feel as they do, but being creatures of habit, they persist in emotional patterns that are not good.

One such person was Eilene. In her mid-fifties, she described herself as "beyond burnout." She came to counseling on the heels of divorce explaining that her niceness had finally caused her own undoing. "My relationship with my ex-husband was about as lopsided as it could get," she told me. "I was constantly trying to figure out how to keep him in a good mood and he was constantly complaining that I never did a good enough job keeping him satisfied. We had one of those situations where I did almost all the housework while he drank beer in front of the TV. I never felt like he gave me the respect due me, but maybe he didn't because I didn't really show him that I respected myself."

Most people would not have suspected Eilene to be the "weak-kneed" kind of person because she had established quite a reputation in years past as a reliable worker who had few enemies and many friends. She had begun her career as a grade school teacher, and had eventually earned her master's degree in administration. Only recently had she retired from the educational field and was now leisurely looking for something of interest to occupy her time. Very few people knew that at home Eilene had lived with sadness and futility because of an unhappy relationship with a husband who could rarely be pleased. Now as a new divorcee, she was trying to make sense of her life, and part of that included an examination of how things had gotten to the point where she felt more emotionally drained than ever before.

As Eilene talked more with me I learned that she was the quintessential people pleaser. Formerly married to a very controlling, self-oriented man, she had played right along with his demands because she had constantly assumed that she could not afford to stand up for what was healthy and right. If, for example, her husband went out at night to meet friends, he would not feel it necessary to tell her how to get in touch with him. "I'll let you know where I am when you need to know," would be his reply.

"How would you respond when he showed no regard for reasonable accountability?" I asked.

"Well, I didn't have much choice but to let him go and deal with it by myself," Eilene replied with a shrug. When I told her that I knew plenty of wives who could not sit idly by wondering what kind of mischief their husband was up to, her response was, "Yeah, but they weren't married to Walt." She had convinced herself that his insensitive behavior required her to accept as normal the feelings of unworthiness and despair that she had carried for so long. Though she had been second to none in her educational career, she had never translated the firmness she used at school into her home life.

How about you? Have you ever found yourself in relationships that kept you bound to unwanted and unhealthy emotional pitfalls? If you have, it's time to give yourself permission to shed the debilitating feelings, exchanging them for more reasonable responses. To do so, you must first recognize the harmful emotions that you carry, then identify the alternative responses anchored in the healthier patterns of thinking. In this chapter, we will examine the need to set aside at least three unhealthy emotional responses: false guilt, paralyzing fear, and anxiety.

Exchanging False Guilt for Self-Worth

"To err is human." Never has a more true thought been stated than that. No human can come close to claiming perfection. One starry-eyed woman once told me, "I suppose my mother makes mistakes just like anyone else, but I don't know of any. She's as close to perfection as anyone you'd know." Either this woman had a neurotic need to see her mother as perfect so she could feel special due to her connection to such an angel, or the mother had done a poor job of revealing who she was—or maybe both. Suffice it to say, no one can claim perfection or anything close to it.

Every person is guilty of some misdeed. We each have traits or behaviors that point to some flaw within the personality. This is not a flattering notion, but it is true nonetheless. If you are human, you have something for which you could feel guilty. Some of your guilt will be the result of minor errors in judgment; some of your guilt may be anchored in more severe matters.

Healthy individuals are fully aware that they have shortcomings and they make no particular effort to hide that fact. When they do something wrong, they admit it, they recognize specifically what they did wrong, they choose the better alternative, and then they move on. In short, they practice true guilt, the acknowledgment of blameworthiness that then leads to a constructive and freeing response. For example, the husband who speaks insensitively to his wife will admit the error of his words or attitude; he will seek forgiveness and if needed, restitution; he will learn from his mistake by choosing to change his insensitive ways; and then he will move forward with no further reason to feel guilty. In such an instance, true guilt served its proper function.

People pleasers tend not to operate with true guilt. They too commit errors, but instead of making the necessary adjustments and moving on, they tend to wallow in the emotion well beyond the point of constructive change. They receive upon themselves ongoing judgment and condemnation, resulting in a powerful need to prove that they should eventually be allowed to be forgiven, but never really believing that to be possible.

Does false guilt apply more to you than true guilt? If so, you are likely to convince yourself that you deserve to be looked down upon and that the only way you might be deemed OK again is to somehow pay enough penance to bring your debt up to even.

Look over the following statements common to people who struggle with false guilt. Put a check by the ones that often apply to you:

_____ 1. I feel I should make up for my mistakes by proving that I'm really a good person.

_____ 2. It seems that I apologize more than necessary.

_____ 3. Somehow I don't feel that I compare well to others.

_____ 4. When someone tells me I'm forgiven, I still may not feel forgiven.

_____ 5. I'd rather not let people know the real me because they may not like what they see.

_____ 6. When someone else is judgmental, it really affects my mood in a negative way.

_____ 7. It seems that my own wrong deeds are worse than the same wrong deeds of someone else.

_____ 8. I'd be embarrassed to tell even my closest friends my worst secrets.

_____ 9. I can place some very strong demands upon myself regarding how I'm supposed to act.

_____ 10. I feel as if few people really would accept me if they knew my frailties.

It's normal for you to struggle with the emotion of guilt since it is rarely handled by people in a perfectly clean fashion. If five or more of these statements describe how you feel fairly often, it is probable that false guilt has a grip on you. The more you contend with this emotion, the more likely it will be that you delve into people pleasing as a way of buying the credibility your false guilt will not allow.

"That really hit the nail on the head for me," Eilene said as we discussed her propensity toward false guilt. "I'm forevermore feeling like I've got to prove myself. It's like my mistakes are magnified twice as large as anyone else's." She gave me an example of a time several years prior when she made the decision to go back to college and complete her master's degree. "Walt made me feel like I was being the most selfish person who was abandoning my every duty because of the time commitment involved."

"Well, were you being selfish?"

"I don't think so, although I did have less time to dote on him and our one son who was still living at home at the time. I got my responsibilities taken care of even while I was taking classes."

"So you finished your degree?"

"Yes, but it was a miserable experience. I had always wanted to go into administration at school, but he made me think I was being haughty for wanting to advance. It seemed like my motives were questioned whenever I would make a decision to improve myself." Then sighing, Eilene continued, "He sure didn't seem to feel too guilty when he traded me in for a new woman, so why did I feel so guilty about trying to improve myself?"

Why, indeed. Eilene was doing nothing immoral or irresponsible, so she had no reason to hold to any guilt, but false guilt had gotten such a grip on her that she had felt odd about branching out to become the unique person she wanted to be.

Such an emotional burden is caused by an inappropriately low understanding of personal worth. People pleasers like Eilene mistakenly allow their sense of worth to be determined by the pronouncements of fickle people who are operating from a less than objective frame of reference. Walt, for instance, did not like his wife attending college simply because he wanted her home to perform her wifely duties (translated, "my maid"). In his disgust for her decision, he treated Eilene in an unworthy manner and she was repeatedly willing to receive his devaluation of her as truth. As long as she bought into this form of thinking, it made sense to try to appease him so he would reconsider his judgment and give her a higher score.

Claiming Your Inborn Worth

Let's acknowledge that worth is not contingent upon the opinions of human judges who are driven by their own insecure or selfish motives. Worth is a graver matter than that, and its presence in a person's life is to be left in the hands of the one who gives life, God himself.

Think of the disgust you feel when you hear a news story about an infant who has been abandoned at birth. When you hear of a person putting a baby in a garbage dumpster or leaving the child to die in cold, frigid conditions, what is your reaction? You want to shout, "What is wrong with you!? How could you do that?"

Why do you have such a visceral reaction to such news? It's very basic. At the depths of your being you harbor the notion that life has value. Though you know that the abandoned infant has accomplished nothing to "prove" personal value, you nonetheless cling to the conviction that human worth transcends performances or appearances. Whether or not you ascribe this deep thought to the spiritual realm, you are assuming that by virtue of an individual's created status, that baby has innate worth that no human can rightly ignore.

Now personalize this notion of innate worth. You were once an infant who had achieved nothing, yet you were recognized by someone at the beginning of your life as worthy of love and respect. Through the years you have accumulated a scorecard of deeds that some might deem as good and some as not good. Over and over people have taken upon themselves the position of God as they have responded to you either as one who possesses value or as one who does not. Think carefully: Does the pronouncement of judgment by humans eventually change what we know intrinsically to be true about the value of every human? No. That judgment is not a reflection of your worth at all. If anything, it is a powerful commentary regarding the erroneous thinking that achievements and accomplishments eventually become a more important factor than God's initial gift of worth. Let's affirm that worth is an inherent trait that you possessed on your first day of life and it continues to be a part of you until the day you die, irrespective of your level of achievement or others' judgments.

When I talk with people like Eilene, I challenge them to ponder the question, "Do you choose to let a fallible human have the power over you that belongs only to God?" In her case, she had to come to terms with the understanding that Walt continued to heap guilt on her wrongly because he was actually hoping to build his own frail ego at her expense. Only as she came to accept the undeniable truth that she had been given worth on the day of her birth that no human could deny—only then would she be able to shed herself of the false guilt that held her captive to her non-productive people-pleasing behavior.

Exchanging Fear for Inner Trust

Running parallel to false guilt is fear, an emotion of apprehension that causes persons to assume that harmful experiences are inevitable. People who live in fear often have pessimistic notions about the things that are going to affect their quality of life, meaning they allow uncertainty and doubt to gain a foothold in their thinking.

We often have a stereotyped notion of fearful people which causes us to think of them as "scared rabbits" who tremble at their own shadows or who let paranoia lead their way of relating. While this stereotype may occasionally prove accurate, fear is not nearly that one-dimensional, and what is more, it can be experienced by people who do not readily show outward signs of being fearful at all.

The easiest way to detect the presence of fear in a person's life is by observing the tendency toward defensiveness. Fearful people (whether consciously or not) tend to have their guard up more powerfully or frequently than is necessary. Not satisfied to assume a "take me as I am" approach toward life, they have an inner sense that something or some-one "out there" is going to make life miserable. Because of this, they have difficulty in maintaining a feeling of true openness or confidence.

To get an idea of how fear might be present in your personality, look over the following statements and put a check by the ones that fairly often apply to you:

_____   1.   Too often I tend to explain my reasoning for doing what I do.
_____   2.   If someone might be displeased, I feel I need to have a good excuse for my behavior.
_____   3.   I will alter my plans if it seems obvious my decisions will cause someone else to feel frustrated.
_____   4.   When my ideas seem too separate or unique, I will question the validity of my own thinking.
_____   5.   I tend not to trust my own judgments as strongly as I should.
_____   6.   Too often I shape my behavior to fit what I think others want me to be.
_____   7.   I avoid conflicts.
_____   8.   Too often I won't speak up because my opinions will only create unwanted tension.
_____   9.   Other people don't often get to see the real me.
_____   10. I have had fairly significant bouts with feelings of uncertainty or doubt.

If you checked a few of the items, don't worry; we all have some moments when fear can show itself. If you checked at least five or more of the statements, there is a good possibility that fear grips you more often than is necessary.

Can you see how the presence of fear leads to unhealthy people-pleasing behavior? Just as guilt caused Eilene to be controlled by Walt's judgmental spirit, so did her fear cause her to approach circumstances with doubt and defensiveness. "I can't tell you how many times I would feel like I had to justify my actions or rationalize my decisions," she told me. "It seemed like everything I did was called into question. It got to the point where I constantly doubted my decisions. I had no confidence at times."

"How did your fear cause you to get caught in your people-pleasing pattern?"

"Well, it seemed like I was two different people at times. When I was around friends who liked me, I could be easy-going and confident, but when Walt was in the picture, I'd become more reserved and cautious. Around Walt, I altered the way I acted because I was afraid of the very predictable criticism or rejection he'd give me if I strayed too far out of the mold."

"That doesn't sound like a very happy way to live."

"It wasn't. I never knew when I'd foul up next! It got to the point where I was second guessing myself constantly. Everything I did had to be calculated so that it wouldn't upset Walt." Then shaking her head, she reflected, "Looking back, I wish that I could have given myself more permission to be me, but I guess I was afraid that being me just wouldn't cut the mustard. I was afraid of my own uniqueness."

Can you relate? Have you had experiences when you let fear alter the way you interact with others? You can probably see a direct correlation between this trend and your tendency to live in ways to appease others . . . and you can probably also attest to the fact that fear-based living doesn't work.

The Need for Inner Trust

As you learn to identify the role fear plays in your people pleasing, you may want to consider exchanging your fearful mindset for one anchored in inner trust. This will require you to re-evaluate the necessity of your defenses, choosing instead to approach your world in a less guarded, more confident manner. To begin the exchange process, ask yourself the following questions:

- Is it really necessary for me to justify my behavior as much as I do?
- Can I give myself permission to be unique, knowing that differentness can actually be good?
- Just because someone questions my reasoning, does that automatically require me to alter my thinking or my behavior?
- Can I stand on the conviction that I make decent decisions and that my motives for living as I do are usually good?
- Are there times when I can respond to someone else's skepticism with a firm response of my own, even if others won't fully agree?

My hope is that you can answer "yes" to each of these questions. Your fears can too readily invalidate the things about you that are right and good. As an alternative, you can remind yourself that indeed you are a sound, moral, responsible person whose instincts can often be trusted. The fact that others may indicate that they disagree with you does not have to cause you to let go of your sense of personal trust-worthiness. Can you think like that?

That's what I asked Eilene, and she hesitated as she replied sheepishly, "I'd *like* to think that way, but it might feel foreign at first."

"Eilene, I'm concerned that you have had too many instances when your reasoning was met with a vote of no confidence. As I have come to know you, I have sensed that for the most part your decisions are good, your priorities are quite normal. And even when you make mistakes, you are willing to learn from them and move on. There is much to trust in your character!"

"It sure is refreshing to hear someone say that," she replied, "but I'm afraid I haven't heard that too often."

"The fact that you haven't heard it often doesn't make it any less true. You're ready for a new pattern of living, but the changes in your behavior and communications can't be made until you first direct your mind to dwell on a more accurate and positive pattern of thinking."

As Eilene continued in counseling, she identified several ways she could live with self-trust leading the way:

- When she learned that Walt had criticized her to others, she began choosing not to explain her position; instead she stood on her long-standing integrity.
- When family members suggested that she should rearrange her plans to fit their less-than-necessary demands, Eilene sometimes told them, "I'll stick to what I originally planned."
- Rather than avoiding conflicts, she would hear others out and also calmly state her own positions. She knew she was a fair-minded person.
- When her adult children questioned why she handled circumstances in ways different than their own, rather than fearfully defending her position, Eilene would calmly state her rationale and then allow them room to disagree.

As you consider acting in a more self-trusting fashion, ask yourself, "In what circumstances will I need to apply this better way of thinking?" Be specific. Picture in your mind how fear typically prompts you to behave; then imagine what the more trusting alternative would look like. As you mentally rehearse your better responses, you will be more prepared to act properly when the actual situation arises.

Exchanging Worry for Decisiveness

Close on the heels of fear is worry, which takes your fearful reactions to a level of brooding and ruminating. As you reflect on your incidences of people-pleasing behavior, you will undoubtedly notice how your mood becomes increasingly uptight as you attempt to be all things to all people. A sense of pessimism and irritability can come over you as your mind thinks, "Oh no, what am I to do now?" Worry increases your tension as you then play out various scenarios in your mind. "Should I say this?" "What would happen if I do that?" "Maybe my ideas aren't so good after all." Worry and its accompanying doubt have a way of paralyzing you to the extent that you eventually decide by default just to go along with the other person's preferences.

"Oh my, that would happen to me constantly," Eilene admitted. "Walt used to come home at the same time every evening; so as the afternoon wore on, I found myself fretting inwardly about what mood he'd be in and how I'd handle it if he was in a bad mood."

Perhaps your experiences with worry are not the same as Eilene's, but you've had your moments, too. To get an idea of your propensity toward worry, look over the following statements, checking the ones that would apply to you most commonly.

_____ 1. I tend to ruminate about how I'm supposed to handle potentially tense situations.

_____ 2. I wish to control matters that are ultimately out of my control.

_____ 3. My concentration can be easily broken or distracted.

_____ 4. At times, I feel like I put out increasing efforts with decreased results.

_____ 5. I can struggle with physical symptoms (irregular sleep, upset stomach, muscular tension, headaches).

_____   6.   There are times when I am too concerned about the way I am perceived.

_____   7.   I can feel agitated when things or situations don't fall into place as they should.

_____   8.   My feelings of inner peace fluctuate with the people and circumstances surrounding me.

_____   9.   I spend too much time speculating how events may unfold.

_____   10.   There are times when I get bogged down in unnecessary details.

How did you do? Most people have some experiences of worry, so if a few of these statements apply to you, that is normal. If you could check five or more, it is a good indication that worry can play too prominent a role in your decision making. You are likely not to be true to your own convictions because you are too busy wondering how to keep others from being disappointed in you.

As worry gains a foothold in your emotions, you are likely to be pulled into the preferences or schemes of others since worry does not allow you to follow through confidently on your own instincts. Rather than acting in ways which reflect well-conceived notions, you will instead filter your actions through others' reactions.

The Need for Decisiveness

An alternative to worry is decisiveness. The worrier spends too much time weighing one option against another even in circumstances where the best choice is clear. While it may run counter to your people-pleasing tendencies, you will need to settle on your best instincts and move forward without questioning your every move.

As I spoke with Eilene about becoming more decisive, she nodded her head and she said, "I've been saying most of my life how I'm tired of trying to read other people's minds. Very early I was taught to be sensitive to the feelings and needs of others, but I think that's a lesson I over-learned."

Agreeing, I said, "It's a desirable trait to be attuned to others. There are more than enough selfish people in our world, so it's refreshing to know someone like you who has learned to factor in the needs of others. In your case, though, you've become so consumed with other people that you agonize over your choices and you lose your ability to be firm."

"I'm tired of being uptight. Since Walt and I have been apart and I've had to rely more consistently on my own instincts, I've realized that I've got decent decision-making skills. It feels good to be more of my own person." Pausing, she reflected, "I suppose the real test is going to come as I become close again to new people. We'll see just exactly how strong my sense of resolve will be then."

"Think of it this way, Eilene. There is a reason you have the personality you have and there's a reason you perceive the world in the unique style you do. You are wired the way you are because that's the way God wants you to be. He gave you your personality because He values the unique elements in it. If He wanted you to be like Walt, for instance, He'd have given you the same personality as He gave Walt." Then smiling, I said, "But God didn't do that, did He!"

"Why didn't I realize this sooner?" she asked rhetorically. "I've been so busy trying to match my thinking to everyone else's that I haven't given myself permission to follow through with my own unique perspectives."

"It's wrong for you not to be decisive, because you are robbing people of the privilege of learning from your wisdom and your life's experiences."

How about you? If you have a history of people pleasing, you can surely recall some instances when worry could be replaced with decisiveness. Think of the possible circumstances in which your decisiveness could make a difference:

- *In committee meetings.* The reason there are committees (presumably) is because there is wisdom in drawing upon more than one mind. See yourself as having something to offer in the midst of differing opinions.
- *In marriage.* The reason God made men and women so different is because He wants it to be that way. Be secure in your gender difference, not feeling the need to chronically think exactly as your spouse thinks.

- *With children.* Kids will constantly test the limits with adults, yet they represent minds under construction. They don't need you to cater to their wishes, nor do they need a dictatorial insistence that they should fit your mold. They need a calm, firm voice to teach them to be well-rounded as they learn to blend with varieties of personalities and needs. Be a firm yet calm presence toward children.

- *With friends and extended family.* As you relate with those closest to you, sameness is not the goal. Blending and harmonizing in the midst of difference is the goal. Determine that you can be a team player even in those moments when sameness of thought is not present.

To exchange your emotional responses of guilt and fear and worry for the better alternatives, you will need three ingredients: (1) awareness of the ways your troublesome emotions are displayed, particularly their subtleties; (2) a firm grasp of how the better alternatives will affect your communications and behaviors; and (3) a commitment to enacting healthy choices.

The more miserable you are with the poor results of excessive people pleasing, the more motivated you will be to make the necessary adjustments in your emotional and behavioral patterns.

For Personal Reflection

When can you know that guilt is a right and appropriate emotional reaction?

_____

_____

_____

_____

In what circumstances do you accept guilt that is false or unnecessary?

_____

_____

How would your life change if you chose instead to act consistently as a person of God-given worth?

In what ways do you defend yourself unnecessarily?

If you chose to trust your instincts more consistently, how would this help you be less of an appeaser?

In what ways would your quality of life be improved if you chose to act more decisively?

In what ways would your efforts to be a true servant improve if you chose not to get hung up in reactions of false guilt, fear, and worry?

_____

_____

_____

_____

How the People-Pleasing Pattern Is Formed

Chapter 4

A History of Anger Turned Inward

While people pleasers like Anita or Tommy or Eilene differ greatly in the ways their behavior is displayed, there tend to be common reasons why they act as they do. One of the chief causes of imbalanced people pleasing is a mismanagement of anger.

You may wonder, "What does anger have to do with people pleasing?" The answer is, "Lots!" The best way to recognize the links between anger and people pleasing is to gauge the residual frustration felt by these persons as they engage in ongoing efforts to satisfy everyone else. As Eilene put it, "It's crazy to think that I work so hard to keep everyone in my life happy, and yet I'm frequently unhappy inside."

Can you relate to that statement? Keeping in mind that people pleasing is usually accompanied by the "requirement" to be dishonest, most of these people cover up any hint that they might feel agitated toward others' pushy preferences or insensitive behaviors. In fact, many people pleasers cannot be honest with themselves about the hidden anger. For instance, Tommy referred to the fact that he hated his job, yet when I asked about the anger in his life, he claimed to have none. Yet how could he hate if he was devoid of anger? Despite denials, frustration, annoyance, resentment, and disillusionment build inwardly. These are all indicators that anger is being bottled up in an unhealthy way.

So let's begin with a simple question: "Is it ever right to communicate anger?" While most people will give the obvious answer, "yes," it does not necessarily translate into action. Let's take it a step further, "Are you being irresponsible when you feel legitimate anger and you do not act upon it in a timely fashion?" Again, the answer is "yes," but it can be difficult in real life for people pleasers to think of the communication of anger as a potentially responsible act.

From the earliest years, most people develop an image of anger as a despicable or a distasteful emotion—and for good reason. Anger is so often misused and abused that it is easy to conclude, "I don't think it's a good idea to participate in the kind of behavior that anger dredges up."

As I discussed with Tommy how he would constantly drop his projects to solve everyone else's problems, he recalled how anger was poorly handled in his early years. "I was the youngest of four," he explained, "so I had the advantage of observing what did and didn't work with my older siblings. I had two older brothers who were constantly bickering with each other, and I'd watch as my parents mixed it up with them. My dad could be a friendly guy most of the time, but when his anger fuse was lit, watch out! He'd lay into my brothers verbally, and as they got older my brothers would dish it right back. My mother would get all upset and she'd try to bring reason to the situation, but in the end she'd get all flustered and would leave the room crying."

"So how did all this affect you?"

"Oh man! I learned real early to keep my big mouth shut and stay out of the way."

Tommy's early "lessons" regarding anger management are quite typical of folks who later become people pleasers extraordinaire. Realizing that anger can become volatile very quickly, they keep their feelings and perceptions carefully hidden, choosing to be compliant and friendly in order to rise above the fray.

Eilene, on the other hand, had a different early history with the emotion of anger. "My mother was the sweetest person you'd ever know. Daddy wasn't the easiest person to get along with because he really didn't like to talk much and he just didn't want to be bothered. She told me countless times that the best way to clear up conflicts is not to get involved in the first place. 'Don't stick your nose where it doesn't belong' is what she told me repeatedly. She made it her goal in life to be the calming presence wherever she went and I learned very early to do the same thing."

"Did you or your mother ever feel frustrated because of your dad's closed nature?"

"Oh, all the time. But Mom said it wouldn't do any good to talk about it because that's just the way Daddy was." Then she added, "I carried that same thinking into my marriage to Walt. I just assumed that confronting him or trying to make him understand my needs would get me nowhere. Being compliant is what I'm best at."

While Tommy and Eilene took different paths, they had arrived at a very similar conclusion: "It is better just to swallow your anger and keep everyone happy." And both were experiencing similar emotions as a result: depression, bitterness, tension, frustration, impatience. Their good intentions led to unrewarding results.

How about you? Do you have a tendency to be dishonest about the extent of your anger? (By the way, when I speak of anger I include frustration, disappointment, disillusionment, annoyance, and the like.) The deeper you move into the people-pleasing role, the more likely it is that you have a commitment to hold your anger in even when it may not be good for you or your relationships.

To get an idea of how you might be caught in patterns of holding back your anger, look over the following statements and put a check by the ones that would apply to you on a fairly frequent basis.

_____ 1. There are times when I have valid opinions but I don't really speak up.

_____ 2. When someone acts disrespectfully toward me, I may just let it pass without bringing attention to it.

_____   3.   When it's clear that another person feels agitated, I take it upon myself to create a more optimistic atmosphere.

_____   4.   People might be surprised to learn how upset I really feel inside.

_____   5.   Too often I assume that my needs are not as important as the needs of others.

_____   6.   I am too willing to defer to the agenda of others.

_____   7.   Inwardly I struggle with critical or cynical thoughts.

_____   8.   I have had fantasies of running away.

_____   9.   Sometimes I will release my frustrations toward people who are not directly involved in what frustrated me.

_____   10.   It's harder lately to be the friendly person I've been in the past.

No one handles anger perfectly, so if some of these statements look familiar, you're not alone. If you responded to five or more, there is a strong likelihood that you have developed patterns of handling anger that are not good for you. You will need to rethink how you respond to your frustrated emotions, choosing a straightforward approach.

What's Right About Anger

In an ideal world there would be no anger. Every person would be understanding and cooperative and encouraging, meaning there would be no impetus for anyone to feel thwarted or rejected or disappointed.

This is no ideal world. People at their worst can be self-centered and abrasive and condescending. Less severe, they can be innocently unaware of your needs or too preoccupied with their own agenda to notice you. They can feel overwhelmed or they simply may not know how to relate to your personal needs. In such an environment, anger is inevitable.

Anger is spurred because of exposure to the less-than-ideal elements in your life. When someone cuts you off in traffic, you feel annoyed. When you learn that a friend is saying unflattering things about you behind your back, you feel betrayed. If a family member repeatedly interrupts you during a conversation, you feel invalidated. In each of these cases, a form of anger is experienced due to your preference for fair play.

Specifically, anger is tied to your sense of self-preservation. In anger you are wishing to preserve one of three basic matters:

1. Your personal worth. ("Please show me some respect.")
2. Your personal needs. ("Won't you please acknowledge the legitimacy of my needs?")
3. Your deepest convictions. ("I have certain beliefs that I won't lay down.")

Anger has a good function, then, since it prompts you to stand firmly for what is right. This is why the Bible can state, "Be angry but do not sin" (Eph. 4:26). There are times when it is helpful to address wrongs openly, and you can do it without resorting to foul treatment toward others.

People pleasers, however, will experience anger just like anyone else, but they will assume that it is wrong to feel that way, or it is useless to try to act on it, so they will hold it inward. From time to time they may make a few futile attempts to communicate about the legitimate aspects of their anger, but as soon as opposition rises against it, they back down, going into the appeaser mode.

Tommy looked pensively as I spoke with him about the legitimacy of his anger; then he said, "My past experiences with anger have been so distasteful that it seems strange to shift gears and give myself permission to have it legitimately."

"I'm looking at a further development," I explained. "When you tell yourself you'd better not act upon the anger, the emotion doesn't just dry up and blow away. It still remains inside you, but over time it changes its manifestation and takes on different forms."

Tommy was interested to hear more about this, so I gave him an analogy. "In your kitchen you have a trash sack, right?" He nodded agreement. "Suppose at the end of the day you decide you don't like the task of taking the trash out, so you just let it remain where it is. Well, after one day you might be able to let it sit there and you'll experience no negative repercussions." He was with me so far as I continued. "Let's say, though, that three or four or five days have passed and you still have not taken out the trash. Now you've got a couple of problems. First, the trash sack is full to the point of overflowing.

Second, the trash turns sour and begins to smell." He was realizing by then where I was going with the analogy. "The same thing happens when you store up your anger. At first you experience few ill effects, but as days or months or years go by and you continue in the same vein, your emotions sour and your legitimate anger then turns into bitterness or depression or cynicism or defeatism."

While people pleasers originally intend to spare themselves and others of the discomfort that can accompany angry expressions, they set up an even greater problem by letting the anger grow into a very unruly underground system of sourness. Is that what you want?

Redirecting Your Anger

In order to avoid the "trash sack effect" of anger you will need to rethink your approach toward your management of this emotion. While certainly you will want to avoid the extreme of letting your anger out through harsh and abrupt behavior, you will also need to avoid the extreme of keeping it bottled inside. Also, if other people choose to respond immaturely to your legitimate expressions of anger, that is not a cue for you to retreat. Yes, you will need to be sensitive to the other person's ability to receive your messages, but you will likewise need to remain committed to the justified aspects of your needs and perspectives.

To get an idea of the way you can adjust your anger management, let's move forward with the understanding that you are free to choose whatever route you want with your anger. In general, you have three lousy choices to make or you have two good ones. Accompanying each choice is a set of consequences. The key to making the right choices is to contemplate the possibility of each choice (even the lousy ones), and then to weigh the likely consequences associated with each one.

Lousy Choice #1: Suppress Your Anger

Up to this point in this chapter we have been majoring on the people pleaser's tendency to suppress, or unnaturally hold in, anger. This option prompts persons to present themselves with phony impressions leading the way. People who suppress anger feel upset or hurt or annoyed just like anyone else, but they are so insistent upon projecting a proper image that they convince themselves that they can ill afford to be real with their hurt or painful emotions.

For instance, Anita, the woman whose husband and father were both easily explosive, told me of an incident that typifies the suppressive form of anger. "Recently I bought a computer software program to help me keep track of our home finances," she told me. "Over the last couple of years I've prided myself in learning the ins and outs of computers and now I can get around on them pretty well. Buying the software was my way of taking my computer usage from the beginner level to a much higher level of functioning."

"You must have felt pretty satisfied by your resolve to make such an upgrade."

"Well, I was," she said frowning, "but it's all backfired on me." She explained that even though she had kept track of the family finances and bills for years, her husband complained vehemently about making the change. "If it ain't broke, don't fix it," he told her as he explained that he didn't want to hassle with consulting the computer every time he paid a bill or wrote a check.

"I told him that using this new program was much easier than he was making it out to be, but he wouldn't hear of it. Finally, I relented and said we'd just stay with the old system if that would make him happy." Then Anita added, "*One more time* I had to just suck it up and do things his way! I get so frustrated trying to maneuver around his moods, but I dare not let on that I'm feeling that way. If I had perfect recall for all the incidences when I held my preferences in check to satisfy him, we'd spend the entire day just counting the number of incidences."

Anita presented herself (at least publicly) as a pleasant, easy-going woman who was as carefree as could be, but beneath the veneer she had a simmering anger that sometimes bordered on rage. Each time she suppressed her anger she gained a short-term reprieve from conflict, but in the long run, she was harming her own psychological balance as that hidden emotion became fuel for a much more sour disposition.

Over twenty years ago an auto mechanic ran a series of television commercials to prompt customers to use his auto tune-up shops for preventive maintenance. His message was simple: If you pay regular attention to your car's routine needs, you'll keep your engine running smoother for a much longer period of time. With each commercial he would sign off with a big smile saying, "See me now or see me later!"

"See me now or see me later." That's exactly the case with anger, too. You can make the lousy choice to suppress your anger, but don't be fooled. Covering it up only assures that it will surface later in a more damaging form.

Lousy Choice #2: Be Openly Aggressive

When most people think of anger expressions, it is the category of aggressive anger that comes first to mind. If anger is defined as the emotion of self-preservation in which you wish to stand up for worth, needs, or convictions, aggressive anger has the added dimension of being communicated at someone else's expense. Notice the insensitivity shown to others in the following examples of aggressive anger:

- You don't like the way a family member has spoken to you, so you respond with an abrupt or sharp tone of voice.
- You disagree with a person's perspective, so you interrupt the conversation with invalidating comments.
- A discussion with another person is not going well, so in a state of futility you allow sarcasm to seep out.
- Others know you to be opinionated to the point of stubbornness.
- When challenged, you can exhibit a mean streak.
- As you express your preferences, you can make open efforts to cause the other person to feel guilty.
- In sifting through interpersonal conflicts, you rebut the other person's position readily.
- There are times when your behavior is pushed along by a sense of rebellion.

Can you see how each of these expressions of anger can inflict unnecessary experiences of discomfort on the other person? Aggressive anger is an attempt to exert power which will ultimately put you in a temporarily superior position.

In some incidences, the users of aggressive anger may actually have a legitimate purpose. For instance, most people who put their anger on such open display can point to another person's rudeness or insensitivity and say, "I was just trying to make a case against that wrong behavior." Indeed, they may have gripes that are valid. The problem is not in the anger itself but in the ugly communication of it. (By the way, let's also acknowledge that aggressive anger can also be caused by blatant self-centeredness or pettiness, so it doesn't *always* have a legitimate foundation.)

Most people pleasers do not use the openly aggressive form of anger often. Being image conscious, they are likely to be more refined than that. However, people pleasers are not completely immune to aggressiveness either.

Tommy told me about an incident that caught his family members completely off guard. He and his family had been invited to a gathering of the extended family at his mother's house one Saturday evening. Because of a previously scheduled engagement, they had to arrive an hour or so later than everyone else. Within two or three minutes a brother said, "What's the problem? Don't we rate any more in your priorities?" At that point Tommy exploded, "What's the deal with you people? Do you just expect me to drop everything and come running every time you whistle for me? I've got news for you—it doesn't work that way any more!" The family just stood gaping with their jaws dropped because such an explosion was so out of character for him.

Rehashing it with me, Tommy said, "You know, it seems that my whole life has been spent jumping through everyone's hoops. 'Tommy do this; Tommy do that.' Well I'm sick of it, and I'm not going to take it anymore. I've spoiled everyone from my wife to my kids to my relatives to my friends, so that they just think they can snap their fingers and I'll just do their bidding!"

Wow! Tommy was on a roll. He hadn't shown this side of himself to anyone for years. I let him talk on because I knew I wasn't going to get a word in anyway. When he finally finished, I remarked, "At the base of what you're saying is a legitimate message for all to hear. It's actually refreshing to know that you're not the saint you try to portray yourself as being. The only shame in this is that you haven't communicated your message sooner and in a more calm, straightforward fashion."

Tommy was genuinely caught off guard by my modest response because he was certain I would chastise him for feeling angry. While I wanted to teach him a cleaner method of managing his frustrations, I also wanted to let him know that we could still find something reasonable in the midst of his feelings to build upon.

Most people pleasers view anger in "all or nothing" terms. "Since there is nothing good that typically comes from angry expressions," the reasoning goes, "then all anger is to be avoided." I encourage them to modify that thinking by realizing that while aggressive forms of anger are indeed the result of lousy choices, the anger itself may have some validity. They can learn to communicate the anger more appropriately while remaining true to the purpose of the emotion.

Lousy Choice #3: Utilize Passive-Aggressive Forms of Anger

Keeping in mind that aggressive anger is communicated at someone else's expense, let's acknowledge that it is not always exhibited through loud, abrupt means. It is quite possible for aggression to be displayed in a more quiet, behind-the-scenes fashion. Passive-aggressive anger can be far more subtle than open aggression, and it has the "advantage" of allowing the angry person to exert control with the least amount of vulnerability.

To get an idea of what passive-aggressiveness is, look over the following illustrations:

- Your spouse has upset you with insensitive words, so you go into a quiet-punishment mode, refusing to speak for hours.
- You promise to do someone a favor, knowing there is no way you will deliver it in the time the other person desires.
- You have a history of procrastination.

- You have difficulty being prompt. Time commitments are not always kept.
- You may appear to be interested in the advice someone gives you, but you'll not really follow through with it.
- On some tasks you may give half-hearted efforts.
- When a conflict is possible, you'll make yourself scarce.
- You will encourage others to have a particular impression of you, but behind the scenes you actually think and feel differently.

People who utilize passive-aggressive anger feel frustration as much as anyone else, but because they are pain avoiders, they will be cagey in their use of it. Most of them have learned that open displays of their frustration will be met by some form of invalidation, so they have concluded that they must take the safer, more secretive route.

As you might guess, this form of anger can be quite common in people pleasers. While they usually begin by suppressing their anger, they are unable to hold it inward forever. Anger is an energized emotion, so it won't lie perpetually dormant. It will eventually look for ways to get out. Since these people assume that open anger will likely be met with some sort of disdain, the anger is allowed to take on more subtle forms.

The key ingredient of passive aggressiveness that matches the people-pleaser profile is its dishonesty. In the passive-aggressive form, the communicators of the anger are not required to take open ownership of what they feel. For instance, if Anita's husband confronted her because she had neglected to pick up his dry cleaning as she had earlier promised, she could innocently say, "My day got so busy that I just couldn't get to it." Secretly, though, she may have failed to help him due to the thought, "I'm constantly running his errands for him, so if it's that important maybe he'll learn to quit leaning on me so much and manage his own affairs." Anita's pleasing manner wouldn't allow her to be so up-front, so she let her "forgetfulness" do the communicating instead.

Let's recognize that along with the choices to suppress anger or to be openly aggressive with it, passive aggressiveness is a lousy option because it ultimately perpetuates ill will in relationships. In the short term it relieves the person from addressing uncomfortable conflicts, but in the long run it only breeds dissension and manipulative patterns of interacting.

Good Choice #1: Be Assertive with Your Anger

In the 1970s the word *assertive* was the popular psychology buzz word much like *codependency* was in the '90s. When explaining assertiveness, many instructors seemed to indicate that you should just say whatever is on your mind in a forceful fashion, and if others didn't like it, that would be too bad for them. I thought then and I continue to think today that such a description of assertiveness is way off base. An "in-your-face" form of communicating anger is not assertive, but aggressive.

Assertive anger is typified by preserving personal worth, needs, and convictions *while also* displaying a respect for the other persons involved. Assertiveness includes a firm manner of speaking or behaving *while also* acknowledging others' dignity. Even in the midst of decisive communication, assertive people can still be gentle or calm or polite. (This is the anger without sin mentioned in Ephesians 4:26.)

Notice the combination of both firmness and respect in the following illustrations:

- When you discipline a child, you can explain the consequences for both right and wrong behavior, enacting the consequences when necessary without harshness or condescension.
- If a family member criticizes you for a decision, you may decide nonetheless to hold your ground without also getting drawn into a fruitless argument.
- If you are asked to do a friend a favor, but you don't really feel compelled to do so, you can kindly decline without having to give elaborate excuses for your decision.
- When someone does something to disrupt your day, you can explain in an even tone of voice what your alternative preference would be.
- When others act defensively toward your suggestions, you are not required to engage in verbal sparring. Let the person be defensive while you stick to your beliefs.

- Rather than altering your plans to fit someone else's agenda, you may calmly decide to stay the course of your own agenda.
- Even if someone dislikes your schedule priorities, you can stick to your plans knowing you'll accommodate that person when you are able to get to it.

Notice in each of those illustrations that you can affirm the validity of your own worth and needs and convictions without simultaneously having to negate the validity of the same in others. As you permit yourself to be assertive, you are recognizing that it is not possible nor is it necessarily desirable for you to think and act exactly as others do. You are affirming the normalcy of your uniqueness and you are being responsible to uphold what is right. In addition, through assertiveness you are displaying a commitment to openness and honesty, knowing that such traits will result in much healthier relating.

When I speak with people like Anita or Tommy or Eilene, I point out that assertive anger is communicated with an understanding that it will serve the long-term function of a more rewarding way of life. Then I will point out a common hazard. "When you speak or act assertively, there is no guarantee that others will appreciate what you are trying to accomplish. Keep in mind that human nature can tug us in a selfish direction, so it is predictable that the people on the receiving end of your assertiveness might feel compelled to respond by pushing their own agendas all the more forcefully. Likewise, they may just decide that since they can't control you they'll have nothing more to do with you."

That thought is difficult for people pleasers to digest since so much of their self-esteem is tied up in the approval that comes from others. I point out to them that if they are required to bottle up their real thoughts and feelings in order to receive approval, then they really are not receiving approval at all, but a shaky form of conditional acceptance.

Think of the many times you needed to respond to situations assertively but didn't. In the last chapter we discussed how your people pleasing may be the result of guilt or fear or worry, but there is also another dimension for you to consider. It could be that you have been trained to act in unhealthy ways because key people in your life have not wanted to exert the effort necessary for balanced relationships. Whether it was a parent or a spouse or a friend, these people were attempting to keep you in an unhealthy box because they were acting out their own fears regarding growth and change.

Anita, for instance, realized that her father forced her to be compliant largely because he didn't want anyone to insinuate that he might be wrong. Driven by his own hidden insecurity, he led her to believe that it was not good for her to engage in independent thinking. Through counseling, Anita realized that if she continued her imbalanced people pleasing, she would not only be hindering her own personal growth, but she would have been encouraging her father to remain permanently attached to his own shaky, insecure way of living. She decided that while she could not make him have a new method of relating, she could interact with him more as an adult to an adult, thereby removing herself from the toxic aspects of their relating. She knew that he might initially protest her newfound confidence, yet she also realized that she could no longer in good conscience live by the old rules.

As a result of her new understanding of assertiveness, Anita began making some specific changes in the way she would respond to her husband and her father. For instance:

- When her dad criticized her for spending money for some new kitchen wares, she told him, "Dad, I know kitchen items are not a priority to you, but this was something I wanted to do, and I really like my new purchase." In the past she would have just quietly stewed.
- Once her dad scolded Anita's daughter because she said she didn't want to eat some food that had coconut in it. Instead of trying to say sweet things to patch up the resulting tense mood (as she had habitually done in the past), Anita spoke to her father privately and said, "That's something I've already determined with Melissa, so please respect the decision I've already made."

These forms of communication were new for Anita, and they certainly did not feel natural at first. But she had rightly concluded that it was necessary to be open with her father because the alternative was to sit upon growing amounts of resentment. She was realizing that her excessive people pleasing was actually damaging her emotional well-being and she was harming the future of her relationship with her father by holding in her legitimate perspectives.

To incorporate assertiveness into your own life, you will probably need to rethink some of the old messages given to you by those who would hold you back. Do you really believe, for instance, that your uniqueness indicates you are wrong? Is it true that you can't pursue some experiences that might happen also to be self-gratifying? Does harmony *really* require total compliance? As you grapple with these and other questions, you may conclude that it is not only OK, but necessary to preserve openly the aspects of your worth, needs, and convictions that others have tried to deny you.

Good Choice #2: Know When to Drop Your Anger

There are times when you experience anger, and you have a legitimate reason for feeling it, yet there is no constructive purpose to be served by communicating it. Suppose, for instance, that a coworker is in a foul mood and in the midst of a bad day he forgets to follow through on a task that would have smoothed your day. You may determine that while indeed it is reasonable that you feel annoyed or frustrated, the situation is not of a great enough magnitude to warrant the confrontation, particularly given the fact that the coworker is not in a mood to receive what you have to say. So you drop the anger.

Can this option be a good choice? Yes. Being wise enough to pick your battles carefully can be a sign of maturity. Though others may not always treat you in ways that fully demonstrate respect, your ego need not be so fragile that you are compelled to confront each and every infraction against you. At times, you can determine that the wisest way to preserve your dignity is to choose not to become entangled in losing or insignificant exchanges.

By dropping anger, you can choose instead to:

- Accept others as fully human
- Recognize that your influence over others' choices is limited

- Endorse the value of forgiveness
- Know when not to press an issue
- Prioritize kindness over impatience or irritability
- Live with imperfections
- Be fair in the expectations you have toward others
- Relinquish your yearning to be in control

When you drop anger, you are not denying what you feel. Instead you are yielding to other traits that are of higher value to you: love, acceptance, grace, and the like. The apostle Paul, in Ephesians 4:31–32, instructs us to put away the negative forms of anger in favor of kindness and forgiveness. When you can have assertiveness while also knowing when to let go of anger, that indicates that you are finding the appropriate balance in your pleasing behaviors.

As I talked with Eilene, I heard her make a mistake in judgment common to many people pleasers: "I feel as if I spent years dropping my anger toward Walt, but in the end I only felt more bitterness. It didn't work!" She then gave examples of how she would choose not to say anything when he was in a bad mood, or she would let the opportunity to criticize him pass when she felt he was rude to her family.

I explained to her, "Many people confuse the choice to drop anger with the suppression of anger. When you suppress anger, your choice is anchored in fear and phoniness. You are attempting to project an image that is not accurate. When you drop anger, though, it is anchored in a re-prioritization. By that I mean that you consciously choose to supersede the anger with higher values. You recognize that the anger is valid, but you have other emotional or spiritual or relational goals that weigh stronger at the moment."

For people pleasers to truly drop anger, they first need to be satisfied that they are doing a good job in being assertive when it is truly necessary. Satisfied that they are being true to their sense of worth, their legitimate needs and their basic convictions, they can then determine to move on to options that will be less acrimonious or conflictual.

I told Eilene, "I want you to know that letting go of your anger does not require you to be untrue to your feelings. I get the impression that with Walt you would keep quiet or act compliantly to keep the peace, but that doesn't mean you dropped your anger. I *want* you to feel the freedom to be assertive, to be bold and firm when necessary. I don't want you just to invalidate your self-respecting feelings just to keep someone from being upset. Dropping anger is a choice of love, not a choice of defeat."

How about you? Do you have a strong-enough understanding of anger that you can choose when to be assertive and when to accept imperfect circumstances for what they are? Chances are that you did not receive training in your developmental years to know the meaning of your anger and to sift out the lousy options from the good; but even with the lack of training, you can begin today knowing that anger does not have to remain bottled up inside you, only to play havoc with your relating patterns. Others may not appreciate the healthy choices you make regarding your anger management, but that does not have to dissuade you from making those right choices anyway.

In the next chapter, we will explore further how you may have a tendency to hand over your good decisions to others, and how you can choose instead to reclaim your independent decision making.

For Personal Reflection

When you feel anger, what legitimate messages can it have at its core?

_____

_____

_____

_____

_____

What models of anger management did you have during your formative years? How has this affected your use of anger as an adult?

_____

_____

_____

_____

_____

What experiences have you had that have caused you to hold in your anger, feeling it was of no use to be open about it?

_____

_____

_____

_____

When you suppress your anger, how does this affect you later?

_____

_____

_____

_____

What forms of passive-aggressive anger might you be prone to? Why do you choose this as an option?

_____

_____

_____

_____

In what circumstances do you need to be more assertive with your anger?

_____

_____

_____

_____

How can you maintain your resolve in the event that others may not receive your assertions well?

_____

_____

_____

_____

_____

Picking your battles carefully is a sign of maturity. When can you choose genuinely to let go of your anger in favor of an accepting or forgiving spirit?

_____

_____

_____

_____

Chapter 5

Trained to React, Not Initiate

Occasionally, I will talk with folks who might be called closet people pleasers. By that I mean that they will have many moments of leadership and decisiveness which cause people to assume that they are independently minded, deferring to no one in matters of great importance. Yet there can be incidences when these folks will allow themselves to be pulled into the preferences and opinions of others when hindsight indicates that they should not have let themselves be swayed as they were. Invariably, they can point to key moments when they buckled to outside pressure to conform their thinking to ideas they really didn't agree with. Rather than taking full initiative to act in accordance with their own inner game plan, they turn into reactors, playing off of the cues of a persuasive person who is ultimately enticing them toward something inconsistent with their deepest preferences.

One such person was Richard. In his late forties, he was financially secure and free to pursue only the business offerings that truly interested him. For years he had done well in his sales work, and lately he had been dabbling in small commercial real estate ventures. He was highly regarded by his peers as a man with sound judgment. Involved in both church and civic organizations, he was the type who would predictably wind up in a leadership role wherever he was. People respected him for his long track record of successfully completing the tasks laid before him and influencing people to be their best as they worked alongside him in these pursuits.

"I've got a very ticklish situation I'm having to deal with," he confessed to me. "I've become very close to a woman whom I've been doing some real estate business with, and it's leading me into hot water both on the professional and the personal front."

As he spoke I could tell that he wasn't the type who easily admitted his frailties to anyone. I knew from his demeanor that he was the kind of person who readily commanded and received respect from almost anyone who knew him. If he was in a situation serious enough to seek professional help, I assumed, it must be very awkward indeed. So I said to him, "Just know that I want to help you through the quagmire you're in, so the first thing I'll need from you is the whole story."

Taking a deep breath, Richard proceeded to tell me how he was in a compromised position that he just didn't know how to get out of. The business woman, Karen, had been helping him find locations suitable for small strip shopping centers. Just a couple of years his junior, she was pleasant and outgoing, so immediately Richard took a liking to her. Through her contacts she was able to help him put together one very successful venture, and now they were in the middle of putting together a second deal.

"My problem is that I've allowed a friendship to develop that's beginning to interfere with my marriage," he explained. "We've had numerous occasions to eat lunch together and over the past few months we've even had some evening meals together. I've been sort of honest about it with my wife, but now she's got suspicions that we're having an affair and she's wanting me to break off all ties with her. My wife hasn't always been the jealous type, but she's sure showing signs of it right now."

"You said you've sort of been honest with your wife. How much is sort of?"

"Well, I've told her that she's become a friend and she knows I've had a couple of evening dinners with her, but I've let my wife, Alecia, assume there were other business people with us, but there weren't."

Putting a quick two and two together, I said, "So you've been developing a relationship with Karen while letting Alecia know she was on the scene, but as time has passed you've let a bond develop with Karen that could have some sexual overtones. You know the right thing to do, but you feel paralyzed because you're caught between two women who each have clamps on you but they also have very opposite desires for you."

Shaking his head slowly, he said, "That summarizes it pretty well. I haven't had an affair with Karen, or anything like that, but I'm scared it could happen."

I wasn't one-hundred-percent certain about his affair statement, but I decided to let it pass for now. I knew that Richard professed Christian beliefs, so I asked, "I'm assuming that your beliefs would tell you to walk away from Karen in order to preserve your marriage. So what is it that keeps you from doing that?"

Richard heaved deeply. Again shaking his head he said, "Well, first of all I've got a lot of money on the line with Karen that I can't really afford to just blow away. But second," he paused and I sensed he was inwardly kicking himself, "I'm beginning to question how emotionally stable Karen would be if I told her that my wife was uncomfortable with our relationship. Karen's got a temper and I don't want to set her off to the point that she'll make this thing messy."

In time I learned that there had been several opportunities for Richard to get away from Karen's increasingly manipulative influence, but he had not because he was too committed to his friendly image. Not one ever to cause a scene, Richard had gone along with Karen's suggestions to meet when they both knew it hadn't really been necessary. Though he could be a decisive, principled person in many respects, Richard had a need to be liked, and it was causing him to get pulled deeper and deeper into decisions that could ultimately undo him. In fact, as I got to know him better, I learned that this tendency showed up elsewhere in his life, too. With his wife, his kids, the people at church, people at work, Richard allowed himself to be talked into decisions that were not always in his best interest.

Do you ever find yourself in the same bind? People pleasers can have moments when they truly demonstrate resolve and leadership, yet there can still be situations when they let good reasoning fly out the window, setting aside good initiatives, becoming reactors instead. In order to determine if you ever succumb to this same tendency, check the following statements that might often apply to you:

_____ 1. I will let people talk me out of doing something I wanted to do.

_____ 2. I have agreed to go along with behaviors that really weren't good for me.

_____ 3. You might say I have a need to be liked.

_____ 4. I don't always reveal my thoughts fully when I sense it might lead to an argument.

_____ 5. There have been times when I have felt used or manipulated by others.

_____ 6. Sometimes I smile about things even though I really don't need to be smiling.

_____ 7. I'd rather just go along than have to work against a stubborn, hard-headed person.

_____ 8. Sometimes I hesitate to be as trusting of my gut instincts as I probably should.

_____ 9. Though I have strong ideas, when I develop a personal relationship with someone, my relational desires may outweigh the strength of my ideas.

_____ 10. My moods can be keenly affected by the moods of others.

We all have moments when we filter our decisions through someone else's grid, so it would be normal for you to respond to some of the statements. If you could check five or more, it could indicate that your reactions to others may outweigh your initiatives. You will need to be careful not to let your life be too easily molded by someone else's desires for you.

A History of Dependency Imbalances

When I talk with people like Richard, I begin watching for the ways dependency plays out in their key relationships. Many people, like Anita or Eilene, can relate immediately to the word *dependency* because they see themselves often in a position subordinate to a strong-willed controller. Natural leaders like Richard, however, may have a harder time admitting to this trait because they wrongly stereotype dependent people as weak and wishy-washy. Since they are not this way, they may assume the quality is in others but not themselves. This can be erroneous.

Dependency, in the emotional and relational realm, can be defined as the tendency to allow your mood or inner sense of direction to be determined by outer circumstances. When you set common sense initiatives aside, or when you allow your good instincts to be overruled by emotional considerations, you are at that moment in a dependent mode. You are letting the outer world have strong sway regarding your inner mission.

Let's stay balanced: Is it always bad or wrong to be dependent? The answer is no, because this is a trait common to every person. On the day you were born you displayed your dependency by crying, wanting to be held and affirmed. As others nurtured you and responded to your need to feel valued, you calmed down. Inwardly you felt satisfied because your outer world had stroked you. This yearning continued in the months and years to follow, and in fact it remains in you to this day. No sane individual is so thick-skinned or emotionally independent that they are completely unaffected by the desire to be openly affirmed.

We live interdependent lives, which means our actions and decisions are frequently going to be intertwined with the needs and preferences of others. Successful people, in fact, realize the value of factoring in the perspectives of others and learn to read others' moods in order to maintain a team mentality in their decision making. They allow their decisions to be affected by others, not because they are spineless or fearful people who live too cautiously, but because they know the necessity of harmonizing many differing sets of needs and goals.

The problem facing people pleasers, then, does not lie in the fact that they are dependent, but that they have not learned to keep their dependencies properly balanced. Richard, for instance, chuckled as he said, "Up until you mentioned it I never would have pegged myself as being someone with dependency issues. I've always been popular, so people have just naturally gravitated toward me to get my thoughts on a number of matters. If anything, I have had moments when I felt I was too depended *upon*, but not too dependent."

"The fact that others have depended on you doesn't take away the reality of your own dependent state," I explained. "In fact, many leaders depend upon others to depend on them—that's how they learn to feel good about themselves." Richard nodded because he knew first-hand what I was talking about. I continued, "Over time, patterns develop in our relationships where we subconsciously feed on one another as we make our decisions or as we allow relationships to unfold. You're not openly thinking about it, but quietly the need to feel connected or approved can cause you to take on a reactor's approach to life. You do what you do in order to impress or gain the approval of someone who has taken on a significant role to you in that moment."

Richard, for example, had prided himself on being a good provider for his wife and kids, but through the years he had felt a distinct lack of appreciation from Alecia. He had become hypersensitive to any critical statements she'd make, and though he had not planned it to be so, he began noticing more when women showed respect toward him. When Karen came along, he had let his guard down long enough to let her gain an emotional foothold in his decisions. By the time he came to my office, the pattern had emerged whereby he tried to keep Karen impressed, so he would go along with her desires, even when it ultimately ran counter to what his instincts told him was good for him. Richard's normal dependency needs had become imbalanced to the point that he was living less on his own well-conceived initiative and more in reaction to Karen's desires.

To regain his sense of direction in his life, Richard needed two things: (1) a feeling of emotional competence, and (2) a renewed mission for who he really wanted to be. Let's look at each of these separately.

The Need for Emotional Competence

Invariably when people pleasers are pulled into someone else's plans, it is through the emotions that they are hooked. Whether it is through fear or guilt or the yearning to be liked, these people can lay aside the logic that might apply to the circumstance and let their feelings guide. Richard, for instance, chose to have dinner meetings with Karen, not because it made good sense to do so, but because he enjoyed the thrill of having a stimulating woman pay attention to him. In the case of Anita, she was super-accommodating to her husband, Ted, not because she reasoned it to be a good way to live, but because she didn't have the emotional strength to hassle with his easy irritability.

Since emotional tugs play such a vital role in the over-development of people pleasing, it would stand to reason that there need to be well-developed skills in knowing how to set the course for your own personal direction with a special emphasis on the role of emotions. Now think about this: When you were young, how many times did someone sit down with you for the specific purpose of addressing the way your emotions factored into your decision making? If you are like most people pleasers, it happened far too infrequently, if at all.

In Richard's case, his parents discussed emotional matters with him on very rare occasions, and when they did, it was more for the purpose of telling him what not to do as opposed to helping him learn to claim direction to his emotions. He told me, for instance, of a time when some fellow teenagers talked him into doing some pranks one weekend that eventually got him into trouble with some neighbors. "Son," he was told, "I don't know what kind of thrill you were expecting when those boys talked you into going along with their pranks, but I can tell you, whatever jollies you planned on finding aren't worth the heartache you'll get once your actions find you out."

Richard explained, "That's about as far as we'd get when we would talk about emotions in my home. My dad might go so far as to acknowledge that I wanted to feel thrilled, but we'd never really delve into why I felt as I did, and we sure didn't discuss the meaning of my emotions on any deep level."

Does that sound familiar to you? Most developing children receive a quick reference to their emotions with little or no real instruction associated with it. For instance, you may have heard something like:

- "I don't know why you're in such a bad mood, but you'd better get over it quick!"
- "Crying's not going to help matters any."
- "If you'd quit feeling so sorry for yourself maybe you'd learn that things aren't so bad after all."
- "What's got you so angry? There's nothing you can do about it now."
- "If you're feeling so guilty, that means you must've done something wrong."

If emotions were addressed at all, they were probably done with the purpose of getting them out of the way as quickly as possible so you could move on to less bothersome matters.

Think of the many subjects that have an emotional nature to them, and think of how much careful guidance you needed in order to know how to make your way through them. For instance, as a developing child and teenager you needed the instruction in these areas and many more:

- The establishment of inner peace with a balance of true humility
- How to determine when to be assertive with your anger, even among difficult people
- How to respond to the rejecting messages others would give you
- How to maintain a balance between being accepting and being principled
- Knowing the difference between true guilt and false guilt
- Knowing how to handle your first experiences of "being in love"
- How appropriately to let someone know that you feel hurt or disappointed
- The ingredients necessary to keep worry from gaining a stronghold in your personality

Now think carefully. How often did key people challenge you to grapple with your own ideas regarding such subjects as these? When I posed that question to Richard, he grinned as he answered, "Counting the next time, that will be one. We just didn't talk like that where I grew up." Of course, he's nowhere near being alone in that regard. While training regarding emotional direction is needed in dire ways, many can echo Richard's words as they acknowledge that they had no training to be emotionally competent.

Now consider what happens to a person when there has been very little training regarding emotional matters. It is easy to see that these people will defer to outer circumstances, particularly in moments when the nature of their emotions becomes confusing or unpleasant. Richard, for instance, had many experiences in business where he had learned to keep his emotions corralled so he could move forward in a suitable manner. Here he was now in his late forties confronted with conflicted feelings toward his wife while simultaneously having desirous feelings for another woman. In his right mind he knew what he should do, but his lack of emotional strength caused him to flirt dangerously with disaster.

In what circumstances are you most likely to let your emotional direction be determined by outer circumstances? Whether you are with someone who appeals to you because he or she accepts you or whether you are in the presence of an intimidator, you surely have moments when you attempt to satisfy your emotions through some form of unhealthy appeasement. As you recognize those vulnerable moments, think carefully: Do you have the ability to redirect your thoughts and choose a course of action most consistent with your deepest beliefs?

I teach people pleasers that their problem is not the absence of competence in their emotions. They may not have been *trained* to use competence in their emotions, but the competence is available to them nonetheless. Rather, their problem may lie in the tendency to quietly hand over the direction of their emotions to others. This trend can and should be reversed. Think carefully, for instance, about the situations in which you tell yourself that you can't really help the way you feel. Confront your self-talk. Is that really true? Are you truly incapable of taking your behavior in the right direction, or are you merely allowing your behavior to be a reaction to the circumstance in front of you?

Richard thought for a moment as we discussed how he had not taken charge of his emotional direction. "So you're suggesting to me that I really haven't gotten a grip on my emotions with my wife, which means that I'm vulnerable to letting my emotions toward Karen overrule my common sense. Am I understanding you correctly?"

I nodded. "That's exactly what I'm saying. I think you allow way too much time to lapse before you address the choices you need to make regarding your emotions, and over time you subconsciously let your emotional direction be determined for you by outer sources." Then I added, "And that's dangerous."

When you are in a people-pleasing mode, it is easy to make the circumstance in front of you the issue. For instance, you may tell yourself you'd be emotionally fine if that person were more pleasant or more understanding. In fact, though, the real issue to be addressed is your own unwillingness to think through all the options in front of you. As a child who did not receive training to contemplate your emotions, it was predictable that your dependencies would be unbalanced. You are an adult now. Will you give yourself permission to take ownership of where you are going in your primary relationships?

The Need for a Sense of Mission

Once you have determined that you are indeed competent to make good choices in your emotions, it is necessary to tie that competence onto a greater mission. If asked to identify their deepest convictions regarding success and maturity, most people pleasers could give a good answer. Through the years they have learned to intellectualize what they know to be correct, even if that intellect does not always carry over into experience. While they can articulate what a successful life is, their experiences often tell a different story.

Such was the case with Richard. "From time to time I've taught classes at my church, and when I'm standing in front of a group of people I can wax eloquent about the ingredients necessary for a successful life. People like what I have to say and they enjoy my delivery. I've been told numerous times that I've really been helpful to individuals."

"That's got to be gratifying to you," I remarked. "What sort of things do you tend to emphasize when you teach?"

"Well, the part of town where I live is heavily influenced by materialism. People there have the illusion that if you look right on the outside it somehow means you're somebody. My emphasis, then, is to challenge people to consider who they are inwardly. Stripping away the veneer, what really makes you tick? I like to challenge people to define themselves in terms of their spiritual values first, then to translate that into solid relationship skills."

"Sounds great! I can imagine that people really need to hear what you have to say."

"Oh, they do, but so do I! I need to listen more carefully to what I teach because it seems that my own life lately has veered off course. For whatever reason, my emotions and behavior don't always go the direction my brain tells them."

Richard's plight is common among people pleasers. Most of the ones I speak with are not deficient in the intelligence department. From early in life, most have been told what is right and proper. Usually they know that over-compliance or vying for acceptance can be harmful to their way of life, yet they practice these things anyway. Why is this?

The answer lies in the fact that knowing about mature living does not necessarily translate into doing it. Before the intellect turns into a lifestyle pattern, there first needs to be a burning desire to live according to what you know is right.

Let's look back again into your developmental years. Surely you recall some sort of teachings about right and wrong. The "do's and don'ts" of living were not neglected in most people's history. Now think carefully: How much encouragement did you receive to take those instructions and claim them as your very own? To get an idea of what I mean, I explained to Richard, "When you were fifteen or sixteen and really showing interest in the opposite sex, I'm sure you had some sort of teaching about how to treat a woman, right?"

"Well, actually we didn't talk about girls in my home, but I guess you could say I picked up somewhere that I was supposed to be courteous and considerate, if that's what you're getting at."

"Exactly. Now let's take it a step further," I said. "Somewhere along the way you needed someone to challenge you to take ownership of those simple teachings so you could turn them into a more deeply defined code of life. For example, someone needed first to encourage you to take your beliefs about common courtesies and tie them to a philosophy of marriage. You needed someone to show you where that good teaching ultimately would lead you. Second, you needed to be challenged to determine if those beliefs were something you really wanted to stake your lifestyle on. You needed someone to ask what you really thought about the instructions given to you. You needed to feel you had permission to question your instructions until you were satisfied that they were your very own."

Snickering, he replied, "We never did anything close to that."

Only when you grapple on a deep level with the correct instructions you've been given can you take those teachings as your own. Then and only then will a sense of mission or purpose emerge in your lifestyle choices. It's not good enough for a people pleaser to say, for instance, that she knows she should be more decisive when the extended family begins telling her what to do. Rather, she needs to know *why* she would be decisive, and she needs to tie her reasoning to her commitment to a healthy, mature way of life. Then she is not just acting upon good intellect, but upon purpose and meaning.

Do you have a well-conceived sense of purpose about who you are and what you are trying to accomplish with your life? Have you thought how that sense of purpose can remain intact even when others seem to challenge it or attempt to draw you off course? Is your internal guidance system well-defined and strong enough to withstand the stretches in your life that seem dreary or disappointing? If not, you probably do not have a powerful enough definition of yourself. Time (either alone or with a trusted guide or counselor) will need to be spent determining what beliefs you really want to stake your life upon.

Richard had an unsettled look on his face as he told me, "I've never really seen myself as a man without a plan. Particularly in my professional life, I've been very goal-oriented. But I'm realizing that in recent months my behavior has represented a real large question mark upon my life. It's like I'm seriously asking for the first time in my life, 'Who am I?'"

"What you're going through right now isn't the worst thing that could be happening to you," I replied. "I'm sorry you and your wife are struggling with your marriage as you are, and I'm sorry you've felt depressed lately. At the same time, I think you're realizing that too much of your life has been spent reacting and not truly initiating. In fact, during moments when you'd tell yourself that you were highly independent, you still had your eye on other people to determine what they thought about you. I'm hoping you will take this time in your life to reflect earnestly about how you really want to be known. Rather than keeping your finger to someone else's pulse, you can gauge your decisions on what you truly believe."

How about you? Are you also at that place where you are ready to ask, "Who am I?" As you come to terms with that question you will notice a distinct difference in your relating patterns. Specifically, you'll be more inclined to initiate your own behaviors rather than unnecessarily letting your decisions be filtered through the reactions of others. Note in the following illustrations how this could play out:

- When you are asked to do something that sidetracks your day's schedule, rather than letting your day be ruined, you can choose to comply with the request or you can choose to say no, depending on which response *you* know is wisest.
- If someone communicates displeasure with your perceptions, it is not necessary for you to immediately alter what you think. First, carefully weigh what is said, and then respond as you deem best.
- If a person is argumentative with you, you are not required to enter into the argument, nor do you have to retreat in fear. State your beliefs but don't feel like you must make that person agree with you.
- You can be considerate of the needs of others as you choose how you will handle a conflict, yet that does not mean that you will give up your initiatives to do what you know is appropriate.

As you gain confidence in your emotional and relational competence, and as you become more firmly anchored in a well-conceived mission, you will be less prone to being pulled into the priorities others may have that conflict with yours. Instead, you can take delight in the realization that you have different perspectives, and that differentness can be cause for celebration, not degradation.

In the next chapter, we will further explore the roots to your people pleasing as we examine how you may have developed too much of a good thing—your sense of responsibility.

For Personal Reflection

In what incidences do you tend to set aside your own initiatives, letting others determine your course of action?

_____

_____

_____

_____

In your childhood, how were you instructed regarding the meaning and direction of your emotions?

_____

_____

_____

_____

What effect does this have on the way you respond to emotions as an adult?

_____

_____

_____

_____

How would your life now be different if you permitted yourself to carefully contemplate your choices in emotionally tense circumstances?

_____

_____

_____

_____

_____

What key traits would you like to have as the defining elements in your personality?

_____

_____

_____

_____

_____

What circumstances inhibit you from living with those traits leading the way?

_____

_____

_____

_____

In what ways have you attempted to live correctly, but without having a fully conceived sense of purpose attached to it?

_____

_____

_____

_____

Write a mission statement describing the way you would like to conduct yourself in the following areas:

Marriage

_____

_____

_____

_____

Parenting

_____

_____

_____

_____

Work

_____

_____

_____

_____

Church

_____

_____

_____

_____

Friendships

_____

_____

_____

_____

Extended Family

_____

_____

_____

_____

Civic Organizations

_____

_____

_____

_____

Chapter 6

Responsibility Is Overlearned

There is something in me that just cannot tolerate loose ends. When I see a job half-done or if I know about a problem that no one has tended to, it's like my brain kicks into high gear and I can't rest until the matter is resolved." Robert had been referred to me by his internist because he had suffered for years with ulcers. A high-strung man in his late thirties, he prided himself for having a highly successful dental practice. "We take very good care of our patients," he explained. "Lots of other dentists can do the same quality of work as I do on people's teeth, but no one can out-do me in the quality way that I treat people."

I liked what I heard from Robert because I agreed so strongly with his philosophy of treating people right. In fact, in an earlier book I co-authored, *The Significance Principle*, we explain how the right treatment of people in business is often the deciding factor in the profitability of an enterprise. If more men and women in leadership positions could recognize the power of encouragement and respect, business cultures could truly be transformed. Robert was talking my language!

Yet despite the soundness of his high regard for others, something was clearly out of balance in Robert's life. Uplifting treatment of others should not result in chronic ulcers, so I knew we needed to dig to determine how his right behaviors carried him off-track. As I got to know Robert, the reality began emerging that he actually suffered from too strong a sense of responsibility.

It can seem strange to say that some people can actually be too responsible, but in the case of most people pleasers that is precisely the problem. Most have observed that there are far too many people who are willing to take the easy way out of tasks and assignments, and they have rightly recognized that inferior efforts lead to unpleasant consequences. Wanting to avoid unpleasantness, they have concluded, "Well, if no one else will do the right thing, I guess it's going to fall on my shoulders to get the job done."

As I explored this line of thinking with Robert, I learned just how deeply entrenched he was in this notion. "I carefully instruct my staff always to put the patient first, whether it's involving a complicated procedure in the dental chair or something simple like setting an appointment. I know that behind my back my staff will snicker and roll their eyes because I'm constantly checking and double-checking to make sure everything goes the way it's supposed to go. They know that I can't stand it if one person leaves my office dissatisfied."

"That's the way I like to be treated when I visit the dentist," I remarked, "but I'm hearing you insinuate that your philosophy doesn't always produce the personal dividends you'd like. You seem to be paying a high personal price for your kindness."

"You're right. I hate to say it, but there are some people who will never be satisfied no matter how nice you are to them. Just last week I bent over backwards helping a woman who had a complicated root canal, and I mean I treated her like the queen of England, but she left our office angry. When that kind of thing happens it eats me up inside. I know I did my best and I know that she's just an unhappy woman, but I still take it hard." Then he added, "Another problem I have is that I'm too easily affected by my employees' feelings. Even though I'm the boss, I find myself altering staff procedures to fit their idiosyncrasies. Sometimes I do it knowing it's probably not best for our practice."

"Do you notice the same away from your work?"

"Oh sure! Early in my adult years when I began crystallizing my philosophy of treating people with high regard, I realized it wouldn't work if I merely compartmentalized my behavior to fit my business. So at home and with friends I try to remain in the same train of thought." Then almost with a sense of shame, Robert admitted, "I'm not yet forty and I'm already becoming disillusioned as I realize that some people are just users, or they're just plain blind to their own self-centeredness. I know I shouldn't feel this way, but I get tired of sometimes being the lone good guy."

Can you relate to Robert's circumstances? As a people pleaser, you surely have developed, like Robert, a keen sense of responsibility, taking upon yourself the assignment of being a positive presence in a sometimes-negative world. This is a sound philosophy on your part, yet it is also one that can lead to stress and tension if it is carried too far. Think for a moment about some of the many common scenarios in which a person can actually feel pulled under by too strong a sense of responsibility:

- A woman is very conscientious about keeping in touch with her friends' needs, but she realizes that they don't always respond to her in the same attentive way.
- A worker is careful to factor in others' perspectives in his projects, but sometimes feels overwhelmed by the realization that so many people are counting on him to provide the ultimate solutions for their problems.
- A wife and mother "burns the candle at both ends" trying to keep her kids' and husband's needs satisfied. The result is chronic irritability.
- A father freely helps his adult son financially even though he feels that the son has a mind of entitlement and he'll never grow up.
- A couple has to put an elderly parent in a retirement home because of failing health, but they have a gnawing guilt about not keeping her in their home despite the reality that she needs around-the-clock care and cannot be left alone.

The possibilities for an overly-developed sense of responsibility are endless. To get an idea of how you might be prone to this tendency, check the following statements that would frequently apply to you:

_____ 1. I feel uncomfortable pursuing my own plans when I know someone else would rather direct me toward a task of their choosing.

_____ 2. The words *should*, *ought to*, and *supposed to* appear often in my vocabulary.

_____ 3. Even when it's time to relax, I'm wondering what productive thing I could be doing.

_____ 4. I try to anticipate others' needs even before they speak them.

_____ 5. When people ask me to do something, they *know* it will get done.

_____ 6. If someone else doesn't do a job right, I may step in to make sure it's properly managed.

_____ 7. There are times when I wonder if people are taking advantage of my good nature.

_____ 8. Though others may not realize it, I sometimes wonder if I measure up to acceptable standards.

_____ 9. Too often I feel like I'm the one who is supposed to keep others feeling good.

_____ 10. My sense of correctness can sometimes produce a judgmental spirit within me.

Almost all of us can relate to some of these statements. It's not good to be so independently minded that you simply don't care about the concerns of others. If you responded to five or more of the statements, it is probable that the good parts of your responsible nature have been overlearned. You may need to give yourself permission to be a little less helpful.

"I know something needs to change," Robert told me, "but it's going to feel odd to tell myself that I should actually take less responsibility. I mean, do you know how long this mindset has been guiding me? 'Responsibility' has been my middle name!"

"Let's recognize up front that we don't want to go to the opposite extreme of selfishness and carelessness. You've got a good thing going in your life. Balance, not the elimination of your responsible nature, is what we're after."

Could you use more of a sense of balance in this area? In order to put this subject into a broader perspective, let's examine some common ingredients in the histories of overly responsible people. Armed with insight, you can begin making the needed adjustments.

An Overemphasis on Rules

Try to imagine a life with no rules. Suppose, for instance, you lived in a town with no traffic signals where people could drive as they wished. (I shudder to think that it could actually be worse than it already is.) Then imagine that there would be no guidelines for ownership of property or goods. People could take what they wanted whenever and wherever they wanted it. Add to it that children would grow up with no assignments other than to please themselves. We could go on and on with this imagined lack of order, but of course, you realize that such a world would collapse quickly. Chaos and anarchy are not good things. Raw human nature is sufficiently weak that it cannot be trusted in a world devoid of rules.

Order and structure are good and desirable. Not only do they bring direction and predictability to your life, but on a deeper level they foster an atmosphere that upholds human dignity. Rules remind us that self-restraints and submission and service to others are worthy traits. Along with the direction they give, rules curb us against our more base or crass instincts.

As necessary as it is to fend off chaos through rules, the extreme of excessive rules can be equally as distasteful. Think for a moment about how you would feel if every move you made were subject to a regulation. For instance, the rule says you have to get signed permission from an authority each time you decide to sit in your easy chair and read a book. And before you go to the grocery store you have to check to see if it is your turn to enter the store, and you can only buy a specified amount of fruit or meat. Do you get the picture? Rules can be so powerfully emphasized that they can create a feeling of enslavement;

and just as in the case of chaos, excessive rules could also rob you of your dignity.

Balance is of primary importance as rules are sought. It is in the task of finding that balance that people pleasers can err.

Think back to your developmental years and recall how rules were introduced to you. As a toddler the rules were pretty basic: You have to pick up your toys once you've finished with them. You're not allowed to hit your sister. You're supposed to say please and thank you. And so on. As you moved into the school years, the rules became more specific. They addressed matters of social order, getting scholastic assignments done, being a good neighbor, and so forth. In the teen years, the rules continued to mature as you were given structure for new behaviors such as staying out late, how to conduct yourself with the opposite sex, how to juggle an increasingly complicated schedule. Some of the rules covered organizational aspects of your life; some of the rules addressed moral and spiritual dimensions.

Now let's take the instruction of rules to the next level. How often, particularly as you progressed through the teens, did a parent or mentor take the time to discuss with you how the rule was merely the surface matter, that a deeper concept lay behind the rules? For instance, you can say to a teenage girl, "You have to get home from your social outing by midnight." However, do you also add, "Focusing on the time frame of your social life is not my main concern. I'm wanting you to realize the importance of people respecting people. Let's talk about how a curfew can make a difference."

For rules to be balanced they need to be accompanied by open contemplation of the higher concepts behind the rules. As people learn what the rules are, the rule itself is not to be the main focus, but the reason for the rule's necessity should be.

Robert shook his head as he openly admitted, "I can't recall one single time when we talked like that in our home. You have to understand that my parents were good people, but by no means were they philosophers or psychologists. I don't suppose it ever dawned on them to have a deep discussion about the meaning of our rules."

"You're not alone in that part of your family history," I commented. "Probably ninety-eight percent of families are in the same situation."

Then I added, "I'm not saying that family discussions should always resemble a college seminar discussion group. I am saying, though, that rules are put into their proper perspective when the recipients of the rule can feel like they have the choice to think through its purpose. That way they are not just learning to do what is right strictly out of obligatory duty. They are taught to put structure into their world because there are good reasons to do so."

How about you? Can you see how your behavior would have a different motive if you had learned to think more about the principle and less about merely the external requirement? Often I hear people pleasers complain that they act compliantly even when common sense tells them it's probably not the wisest thing to do. When that happens, the rule is being given priority over deeper thought, and the rule is working against their emotional composure.

For instance, Robert told me of a time he accepted an assignment for the area's association of dentists. "I didn't have the time to do what they wanted, and ultimately I don't think I did as good of a job as I should; plus I got behind in my lab work at the office, which meant my family had to pay for my poor decision."

"So why did you take on the assignment in the first place?"

"Well, I just felt that if I'm going to be a member of the association, I'm supposed to do what I have to do for the good of the organization. I've just got this strong sense of duty that I have to be reliable."

While I applauded Robert's desire to do the right thing, it seemed apparent that his deference to the rules overshadowed his ability to put the performance in proper perspective with his business and family needs. His rule-first mentality canceled the permission to *think* the behavior through in its fullest sense. As a result, his behavior was driven by others' external expectations rather than by his own internal principles.

Exposure to Ready Criticisms

When responsibility is overtaught, there is usually an atmosphere of criticism that fosters it. Recall that two of the primary emotions experienced by people pleasers are fear and guilt. Somewhere along the way these people pick up the notion that they are doomed to be poorly judged if they do not act as others would want them to act. They assume criticisms are right around the corner with many of the decisions they are required to make. Their people-pleasing behavior, then, can be understood as an attempt to look responsible, thereby warding off those judgments.

To get an idea of how critical thinking influences people-pleasing behavior, look over the following scenarios. Do any of them strike a familiar chord?

- A wife is constantly trying to anticipate what her husband wants of her. She explains, "When I don't show an interest in my husband's needs, I know he'll get mad and the price to pay will be too high. It's easier if I just do what I need to do."
- An employee goes along with his supervisor's request even though he knows it will be a colossal waste of time. "There's no need to make waves around here because unique thinking only gets you in trouble," he reasons.
- An adult daughter alters holiday plans to be with her parents. "I've got other things I'd prefer to do with my time off, but my parents get bent out of shape if I stray too far from the plan, so I guess I'll just go along," she explains.
- A woman refrains from telling a group of women at her church that she's having marital problems that may be headed toward separation. She says, "I don't dare tell them because some are so staunch in their views about marriage and divorce that they couldn't take the time to listen to my emotional needs."

In each of these situations, the individuals involved are faced with the prospect of going up against opinionated people who will assume it is their job to keep that person in line. While it is good in any family or organization to openly express preferences or needs or beliefs, when those matters are likely to be accompanied by a spirit of judgment, people prone to appeasement tend to go quickly into the compliant mode rather than face the ugliness of condemnation.

Just what is it about a critical atmosphere that spurs people pleasers to assume more responsibility than is necessary? Inherent in any critical message is the threat that you will be labeled as unfit or substandard or ungodly or weak in character. Because people pleasers tend to defer their self-esteem to the pronouncements of others, the prospect of being so poorly labeled is frightening. Grasping for any proclamation of "OK-ness," they will act "responsibly" in order to avoid suffering the shame of being told, "You're no good."

Usually people who succumb to criticism as adults had early experiences in their life's history of responding to criticism with fearful compliance. For example, Robert once told me, "I'm not trying to paint my parents as ogres, because they weren't. My family life was pretty normal, pretty much like anyone else's." He went on to say, "I *did* have to be careful, though, because both of my parents were very opinionated about right and wrong. They still are to this day. I had to be very careful to do the right thing because I didn't want to get criticized and punished just because I didn't think like them. I learned to be responsible, not necessarily because I liked what they said, but to avoid their judgment." He thought for a moment and said, "I'm *still* sensitive to this day when I feel I might be judged or criticized. I'll do almost anything if I think it'll keep someone off my back."

Can you relate? Most of the time when critics make their views known, they can refer to a decent rationale that prompts them to think and respond as they do. (At least to *them* the rationale seems decent.) They are often unaware of the concept of covert messages in their communication. The covert message in a communication is the unspoken but strongly implied insinuation that cues the receiver about what is really felt or believed. For example, in Robert's case, his parents did not always openly say, "You're a bad person if you don't act as we tell you." Nonetheless, that's the covert message he would receive if he strayed too far out of line. In his adult years, he assumed others had the same covert message as they interacted with them, and his need for affirmation was so strong that he would do what he thought was responsible in order to receive (maybe) a favorable judgment.

Actually when you act "responsibly" because you fear being criticized, you are not necessarily engaging in responsible behavior. Instead, you are attempting to read the agendas others have for you, often with complete disregard for the deeper meaning of it all. For example, was Robert being responsible when he chose to run his dental practice to suit his employees? Perhaps yes, perhaps no. It is good for an employer to consider the needs of the subordinates, yet it is also good for the employer to set the vision for the work team, even if it means thinking differently from them. Rather than fearing his employees might be critical of his decisions, to be responsible, Robert would need to run his practice based on his well-thought-out vision of what he felt he should accomplish as a dentist.

During the years of childhood development, people need to learn responsibility that is not driven by a fear of criticism; they need to learn how to assimilate broad perspectives while also maintaining a solid measure of self acceptance. For instance, rather than viewing the differences between himself and his parents as wrong, Robert had needed to recognize that those differences were not necessarily an indicator of right or wrong. Certainly he had needed to be taught good values, but with no fear of judgment he needed to allow for the possibility that he thought . . . well, differently. By making such a distinction, Robert could have chosen his priorities with the realization that responsible behavior is an act of initiative based on genuine convictions, not an act of fear that is intended to appease judgments.

Ideally, then, in his developmental years, Robert's parents would have said to him, "We're going to talk with you about our values and preferences, fully aware that you might not always agree. Know that in your disagreement with us, we'll still accept you as you are. We just want you to think carefully about how you live." Sound too unrealistic? Let's just say that even if your parents did not speak to you that way, *you* can speak to yourself in a manner that expresses self-acceptance even in the midst of differentness.

Unrealistic Ideals

When people pleasers can point to the patterns of rules-based living and sensitivity to criticism, a third element is often apparent as well— the assumption that ideals *must* be attained, even though common sense indicates that the prospect is unlikely. By being too lofty in their ideals, they can take on more responsibility than is necessary. To find balance, they will also need to loosen their grip on idealism.

As an illustration, Robert suffered from the ideal notion that he could treat his patients royally and in the end they would feel satisfied and grateful. When that ideal was not met, he would scold himself, double his efforts, and try even harder. Over and over as he attempted to make matters just right, he would experience aggravation and disillusionment because he could not make people respond in the ideal way.

Numerous examples could be cited, showing how idealism causes people pleasers to take on more responsibility than is reasonable. For instance:

- Parents assume that as they give their kids opportunities surpassing what they had in their own childhoods, the children will be pleased. This results in the parents cramming too many child-centered activities into the schedule, to the point that burnout occurs.
- A married couple once assumed they would be able to talk freely and have a solid understanding of each other. In reality, though, they still don't understand each other fully, so they press harder to make their thoughts known. The result is increased tension.
- A woman prides herself in being a loyal friend, but feels disillusioned as it becomes evident that others don't reciprocate the same loyalty.
- A member of a civic organization is disenchanted because he cannot handle the fact that other members do not carry their fair share of the group's efforts, just as he does.

In each of these illustrations ill emotions are set up because the people pleasers had high ideals for themselves or others that did not come to fruition. The lofty notions they held were not wrong— indeed they were very good—yet they failed to match the reality they faced in their daily circumstances. Determined, though, to cling to the loftiest standards, these people could push themselves to be something that would ultimately not be possible.

Let's affirm that having ideal thoughts is necessary. Even as you admit that your world will not fit an ideal mold, it is still good to aim high. In the meantime, though, it is also necessary to adjust your emotions and behaviors in the event that ideals are not met. This is where people pleasers fall short.

When people pleasers insist upon ideals that are ultimately not going to come true, it represents a form of pain avoidance. Not wanting to face the unpleasant truths about human imperfections, they push themselves to somehow defy painful truths. For instance, though it is true that patients can feel angry toward their dentist, Robert did not want to accept that truth. His ideals led him to wish otherwise. Or though it is true that friends may be inconsistent, or children may be ungrateful, or employers may be unappreciative, or relatives may be judgmental, many people pleasers will push themselves to be super-responsible so they might somehow rewrite those painful truths that they do not want to incorporate into their thinking.

When idealism is too strong, you will notice how easy it is to use phrases like:

- "I just wish . . ."
- "Why can't you just . . ."
- "I can't believe . . ."
- "If only you would . . ."
- "Maybe if I . . ."

These phrases indicate how persons assume if they can just put one more ingredient in place, their troubles will be reversed.

Remember Eilene, the woman who wore herself out trying to satisfy her husband Walt's impossible demands. She once told me, "I kept hoping I would finally do enough right things so he would be pleased with me. Now I'm realizing I would have had a lot fewer heartaches if I had let myself believe that despite my best efforts, I wasn't going to change his disposition. It would have released me from much of the insecurity and pain that I carried for so long." She was beginning to realize that she had been unnecessarily spurred by the false ideal that she could be beyond reproach, thereby changing Walt's critical view of her. In retrospect, now, she could recognize the truth that no amount of appeasement could change a person who did not have the inner conviction to change.

Like Eilene or Robert, you too may decide that it is necessary to factor in the ugly truth regarding human nature. Simply put, people will disappoint. Are you willing to pursue ideals even as you recognize that there will still be loose ends in your life? It would have been helpful if you had received instructions in your youth about the ways to balance lofty goals with aggravating disappointments. You could have been told that it *is* your responsibility to be the best you could be, while it is *not* your responsibility to make others appreciate your efforts and to do likewise.

Even if you did not receive that training in your early years, it is still possible to make the necessary adjustments beginning today. Listen to the signals your personality is sending you through your reactions of disillusionment or burnout or frustration. That could be your personality's way of saying, "Continue to be responsible, but don't continue kidding yourself that you have to pick up everyone else's slack when they choose not to be responsible."

In the next chapter, we will examine a trait that you will need to balance as you continue your efforts to become balanced. That trait is your pride.

For Personal Reflection

How can you tell when your sense of responsibility is too strong?

_____

_____

_____

What is it about the use of words like *must* or *supposed to* that can ruin your motivation to do what is right?

_____

_____

_____

_____

When you take upon yourself the responsibility to keep others feeling happy, how might you go overboard, to the extent that you drain yourself of your own happiness?

_____

_____

_____

_____

Rules can be applied either too leniently or too strictly. How can you know that you have found a balance in keeping rules?

_____

_____

_____

_____

How has your exposure to criticism affected your sense of obligation or duty?

_____

_____

_____

_____

What is the difference between being too idealistic versus being balanced in seeking ideals?

_____

_____

_____

What unnecessary obligations do you need to cease?

_____

_____

_____

_____

Chapter 7

A Very Subtle Pride Is Engaged

W hen you think of a prideful person, what image comes to mind? You probably conjure a picture of a boastful or conceited or haughty person who chronically thinks condescendingly about other people. Sure enough, you would not be entirely wrong in your thinking, because pride can indeed prompt individuals to adopt a lofty view of self that looks down on others. Let me caution you, though, not to consider pride in this single dimension only. Being a very broad trait, pride has a way of displaying itself in a wide array of behaviors, some of them very subtle.

Would you ever think of a people pleaser as one who exhibits pride? At first glance, the thought may seem preposterous since people pleasers, by definition, will set aside their own agendas as they favor the desires of others. That, you might conclude, would indicate very low amounts of pride. In fact, you might assume that people pleasers exhibit large amounts of humility. Maybe this is so, but maybe not.

As you attempt to understand your people-pleasing behavior, be willing to consider that it might be pushed along by some prideful tendencies that are carrying you off the path of healthy choices.

Consider the various situations represented in the illustrations discussed in previous chapters. We have seen through their experiences how people pleasers can experience strains at work, in marriage, with the extended family, and in friendships. In each of the case examples, it seems that the individuals have gone overboard *not* to appear too prideful. These persons often tried to be servants, to consider others more than self, to factor in the feelings of those around them. So you might naturally ask, "What's so prideful about all that? It seems that these people are anything *but* conceited."

To understand how pride can play a major role in people pleasing, let's take the time to consider it fully, and in doing so, let's pay special attention to the ways it can be shown in disguised form.

First, let's recognize that not all pride is bad. Often, you will hear people talk about taking pride in a job well done, or taking pride in their children, in their country, in their complicated achievements. When we speak of pride this way, we are referring to a sense of inner satisfaction, of contentment, and of pleasure. This type of pride can lead to experiences of peace and calm, bringing a confidence into the personality.

Just as any good trait can be overdone, however, pride can cross the line and turn into a characteristic that is very undesirable. In its more troublesome form, pride can be defined as the preoccupation with self's cravings or preferences or desires. Ultimately, pride can include the wish to be in control, to conform circumstances into a pleasing mold. It can cause people to indulge a mind of deservedness, as illustrated by the thought, "You owe me." It can also cause people to indulge hurt and disillusioned emotions as illustrated by the thought, "How could you do this to me?"

Most people pleasers do not exhibit the blatant displays of pride, but they are quite capable of nursing thoughts of self-preoccupation in other powerful ways. To get an idea of how pride might have a subtle yet strong foothold in your life, look over the following statements, placing a check by the ones that would apply to you fairly often.

_____ 1. I may quietly fume when it becomes apparent to me that I'm not being taken seriously.

_____ 2. My nice behavior may be accompanied by the assumption that I should be treated better because of my niceness.

_____ 3. I have struggled with feelings of disillusionment or betrayal because of people who have taken advantage of my good nature.

_____ 4. Inwardly I speculate why people are not as considerate as they should be.

_____ 5. When I witness something good in another person's life, my reaction is to wish for the same thing in my life.

_____ 6. There are times when I'll cover up the real me because I don't want to hassle with others' reactions to my differentness.

_____ 7. I can be calculated in the way I present my thoughts and feelings.

_____ 8. I find myself making more excuses than I really need to.

_____ 9. Sometimes I will pretend to feel something I do not.

_____ 10. I can become worrisome or fretful over my problems.

We can all have moments when pride sneaks into our way of living, so if you could not identify with any of these statements, it would be highly unusual. If you responded to five or more, it could imply that pride plays out in your personality in subtle ways. Though you may be able to keep others from seeing the extent of your self-oriented thinking, it would be beneficial for you to take a hard look at its effect on your relating patterns.

The Negative Side of Pride

It is easy to see pride in some of the more obvious behaviors that reflect some measure of self-absorption: having a critical spirit, interrupting communication, being bossy, being too strongly opinionated, bragging, loudly insisting on your way, acting haughty, being greedy.

But let's recognize that pride can have a more hidden element to it: a person can act selfishly and, when confronted about its inappropriateness, can excuse it as something more innocent than it really is. For instance, consider how some behaviors are less openly selfish, yet they still fit the definition: silent withdrawing, ruminating about someone's flaws, deliberately keeping communication shallow, being closed in self-expression, choosing not to be encouraging, giving a half-hearted effort, procrastinating, staying busy for the purpose of avoiding some-one. Each of these qualities can be spurred by a self-preoccupied motive, but because they are more passive in nature they are not likely to draw attention to their negative meanings.

No human is immune to prideful behavior. We each may differ greatly in the way it is evidenced, but it is a potential presence in every person's life. The reason this can be stated so certainly is that pride rep-resents the core of what is wrong in human nature. Ever since Adam and Eve's choice to defy God by eating of the tree of knowledge of good and evil (in essence, proclaiming their reasoning equal to God's), humans have suffered from raw self-centeredness. To get an idea of its indigenous nature, consider how any infant will act in a self-absorbed fashion. No lesson or training is required to teach a very young child to be selfish. It's so natural that it is a guaranteed inevitability. In fact, when we refer to the possibility of a child maturing, we are referring to that child's willingness to step away from self-centeredness in order to be other-centered. Pride is a quality possessed by all, and only through deliberate choices do we grow out of it.

Whenever adults are trying to make sense of their dysfunctional behavior, it can be useful to question how the environment has influ-enced that behavior, but the understanding of unhealthy behavior will be incomplete without also factoring in human nature's dark side, pride.

Anita was one of the most insightful people I had counseled in quite some time. She knew she had a people-pleasing imbalance and she knew she needed to understand the features that caused it before she could correct it. When I spoke with her about identifying pride's presence in her personality, she nodded her head pensively and said, "I've never been comfortable in assuming my problems were all due to other people's input. I'm smart enough to realize that I'm going to be affected by others' choices, but I've known there is something inside me that causes me to go off base, even when things aren't so bad in my outer world."

I asked her if she could identify the pride which lay at the core of her people-pleasing behavior. She thought for a moment and said, "I can think of a very recent example that might illustrate what you're talking about. Just last weekend I was at my parents' home for dinner and my dad criticized me because he disagreed with something I had told him regarding the way I had handled a discipline problem with one of my daughters. As soon as he jumped my case, I found myself agreeing with him just to get him off my back. I would have said or done anything at that moment just to get him to have a higher opinion of me.

"Now that you're discussing this issue of pride," she continued, "I can see that I was being dishonest with him so I could manipulate him into thinking I was an OK person. I do that sort of thing all the time. I guess you could say that I was so concerned with my own image at that moment that I couldn't allow myself to be real. If I had dropped my preoccupation with myself, I might have been able to tell Dad that we just had a difference of opinion, and I would continue to handle my daughters' discipline in the best way I know."

I smiled as I thought to myself, "Wow, Anita's catching on! She's realizing her own contributions to her people-pleasing pattern, and that's the key ingredient for change."

When people pleasers act subservient or when they defer to others' strong wills, it is tempting to point the finger at the overpowering person, saying, "That person sure is self-centered." That might be a true statement, but to get to the place where change can begin, the people pleaser also needs to look inward, admitting, "My motivations can also be very self-serving. I'm not always an innocent victim." Such stark honesty is not always natural, but it can lead to some major transformations.

Ideally, during your developmental years, you would have been taught to identify the many facets of pride. You would have been trained to recognize that healthy relationships need a good balance between openness and self-restraint, between subservience and independence. You would have been taught that compliance is not always the most loving trait, that sometimes people actually would benefit as you acted decisively and as you occasionally said no.

In most cases, however, developing youths did not receive such training, so quietly their self-preoccupied thinking prompted them to put a strong emphasis on self-protection, even if it meant the relationship would be harmed. Let's add that you may have had some people in your world who made healthy choices so difficult that you were intimidated into remaining compliant. As a youth, you may have had little power to say, "I'm standing up for what is best rather than remaining in a self-protective shell." In that respect, we would say you were relatively innocent as you learned to fall into the patterns of appeasement.

As an adult, however, you are not quite as powerless. As you find yourself pulling into a shell of unhealthy subservience, you can stop and say to yourself, "Wait a minute! My pacifying behavior may produce some momentary peace, but I'm being short-sighted merely for the sake of my own comfort. If I'm going to grow as a mature person, I need to get outside of my narrow world of self-protection and live in ways that are truly good for all who are involved in my life."

Anita smiled at me as she said, "You're sure not making it easy on me. Do you realize how unnatural it would be for me to make the changes in thought that you're suggesting?"

I nodded as I said, "I realize that the most natural style of thought to each of us is to consider what's best for Self. On the surface, your people-pleasing behavior may appear to be very giving or very other-focused; but as you examine it more deeply, you may recognize that you are so intent on meeting your own needs that you will resort to unhealthy measures, if necessary, in order to keep your desires satisfied."

"Prior to counseling, I would *never* have seen this in myself, but I've got to admit that we're really onto an interesting concept," Anita remarked. "I guess what you're saying is that my openness and assertiveness may actually, be acts of humility, and if I'm going to get healthier emotionally I've got to think more along those lines."

I told you Anita was a very insightful person, didn't I!

Choosing Humility over Pride

When I work with people pleasers, one of the most fascinating insights we discuss is how to recognize that some "humble" behaviors are not really humble at all, but self-gratifying. In order to move forward, then, we work to get a good grasp of the concept of pride's opposite, humility. You may discover, as Anita did, that humility may include some dimensions you have not considered before.

The Acknowledgment of Personal Limits

When people allow pride to gain a foothold in their lives, one consequence is that they do not like to acknowledge personal limits. Presuming that they can or should be above common human frailties, they push forward in the attempt to be all things to all people. For instance, pride can cause people not to admit obvious character defects or to act as if they have no insecurities when, in fact, they really do. Being consumed with promoting self's agenda, prideful people find it difficult to say, "I'm limited; I'm not able to be ideal."

Humility, on the other hand, prompts people to admit the obvious: that they are human, and that they have limits. In humility, people can expose their weaknesses or hurts or incompetencies, not because they are shaming themselves, but because they do not want to erect any pretense around themselves. For instance, when a person is asked to take on a very desirable task, in humility that person might openly state, "While that sounds like something I'd like to do, I know that's not my strong suit, so it would be wise to pass it on to someone more capable." Humble people don't mind admitting they cannot be all things to all people.

On the surface, people pleasers may appear to be self-effacing as they put limits on themselves. For instance, a people-pleasing mother may limit her time with friends as she caters to her children, or a worker may limit his time away from the job in order to go the extra mile for a supervisor. Sometimes, however, what you see on the surface may not be a true reflection of the thinking that lies beneath the surface.

It is very common for people pleasers to ignore the reality of their limits as they attempt to give the appearance that they can handle more than they really can. For instance, Anita pushed herself to behave as if she could tolerate her father's and her husband's angry treatment toward her. Over the years, as she tolerated their abrasiveness, she projected the message, "Don't worry; I can deal with all the crud you throw at me. I'll figure out a way to keep the peace." In fact, though, she was not keeping peace, but she was fueling inner tension and turmoil.

"Anita, as you learn to act less compliantly, I want you to realize that you are also admitting the limits of your emotional tolerance. As you let others belittle you with criticisms, you are so caught up at the moment in your own self-preservation that you're not letting yourself be human. You're trying too hard to imply you can handle it all."

"So what do you suggest that I do differently?"

"Instead of just acquiescing the next time your dad gives you unwanted advice about your kids, you might tell him, 'Dad, there's no doubt that you see things I could do differently, but instead of trying to kid you into thinking that I'll always cover my bases with the kids, I need to admit that I have my weak moments. Sometimes I'll miss a few things in my parenting, and I've decided that that's not necessarily disastrous.' In other words, admit your limitations as opposed to trying to make him think you'll correct all your deficiencies."

"Hmm. That would be a *very* different approach," Anita recognized. "But what if he doesn't accept what I say? How do I convince him that it's OK for me to be limited?"

"You don't! That's not your job. You're limited in your ability to force him to understand you—and that's OK, too."

"So I just say nothing?"

"If you have nothing more to say, then, that's right. You have permission to say nothing."

As I was counseling Anita to let go of her people pleasing, I was wanting her to understand that there could be a subtle arrogance when she told herself that it was her responsibility to make her husband or her father feel good about all her decisions. Through her people pleasing, she was indulging the notion, "If I could just act right and speak correctly, then I'd have an increased influence so these people would finally stop thinking poorly of me." That wasn't true! Anita was limited. Through the years, she had proven many times over that no matter how hard she tried, she could not force those two men to change. So instead of pridefully attempting to manipulate their opinion of her, I encouraged her to humbly focus on healthy personal ingredients and to live in accordance with those ingredients, knowing full well those men may never endorse her choices.

"Wow! That's really different from the way I've looked at things before," she remarked. "I never saw the arrogant aspect of my compliance before, but I can see that it's my attempt to control their opinion of me." She breathed deeply as she added, "What a relief to think that I can declare myself to be limited: then I could give up the impossible task of satisfying my critics."

How about you? In what ways are you ignoring your limits? Is your people pleasing really an attempt to subtly control others' thoughts about you? Since you are a finite person with finite skills, why not ease up on your impossible demands and openly admit your limits even if others don't want to acknowledge them.

No Shock Regarding Others' Rudeness

When people indulge prideful thoughts, they talk to themselves about what they should and should not receive from others. "I deserve" is a regular thought that crosses their minds. For instance, when prideful people interact with family members or work associates or friends, they have strong notions about how the involvement is supposed to unfold . . . with them receiving preferential treatment, of course.

Think again about Robert, the dentist who would feel offended by the complaints of his patients. Though outwardly he was very attentive and willing to make whatever amendments were required for improvement, inwardly he would fume, "What's the deal with these people? Can't they appreciate that I'm bending over backward trying to be helpful?" This reaction would eventually lead to problems of bitterness, disillusion, and discouragement. It was as though he was shocked to realize that people could actually be rude or demanding or finicky.

The pride that is associated with Robert's reactions is derived from the assumption that people can and should be understanding and cooperative. While it is hard to argue about the merits of that desire, it is possible that the prideful person can dwell upon it to the extent that it feeds a demanding nature. Although it is right to believe that others should be sensitive, pride can prompt people to cling to a mind of deservedness which then generates inward tension and fretting.

Like Robert, many other people pleasers can feel a shock or they may register surprise when they encounter problems in others' reactions to them because they carry the wish for reasonable treatment too far. To get an idea of how this works, consider the following examples.

- A husband spends the entire weekend doing extra chores for his wife, then on Sunday night he explodes because of the lack of appreciation shown to him.
- A wife feels she goes way beyond the call of duty to be supportive of her husband's pursuits, and then she tells her friend that she can't believe how he just takes advantage of her good nature.
- A man drops out of a community organization because he can't handle the fact that so many of the organization's members expect him to be available, but they themselves are not.
- A teacher is disillusioned about her job because no one seems to recognize the many out-of-the-way things she does to make the classroom run smoothly.

In each of these illustrations, the frustrated persons had legitimate hopes for some measure of appreciation or admiration. The emotional reaction became too strong in each case, though, when the person began thinking, "What's wrong with these people?" or "Why can't they even show a little respect?" Their pride caused them to register inward shock at this behavior.

Humility, on the other hand, makes room for the fact that others can and will act in unappreciative ways. In humility, people can incorporate the ugly truth about human nature, that people are often so absorbed by their own desires that they cannot or will not make room for others' perspectives. In humility, you may still feel a grief about this sad state of affairs, but you will not be shocked.

I spoke with Robert about dropping his shock toward others' rudeness. "I'm in agreement with you that when you act kindly toward others, they should at least have some measure of thankfulness in return. It's hard to argue against such a preference. What I'm looking at, though, is the hidden demand that you carry which requires an appropriate response. It is that demand that leads to your tension."

"So I should act conscientiously with no expectation of any appreciation? Is that what you're suggesting?" Robert wanted to keep his usual calm demeanor, but he was clearly frustrated.

"What other option do you have?"

"Well, I guess I could just quit bending over backward to please people if it's only going to create a shock reaction in myself when they don't respond well."

"That's an option worth considering," I replied, to his surprise.

Humble persons can maintain inner composure because they know in advance not to build their hopes upon something elusive. Without cynicism, they recognize that they can consider themselves fortunate when they receive gratitude from others, but it is not something they hinge their stability upon. As an example, Anita once expressed good insight when she said, "I've geared up my mind when I'm around my dad to expect that he can easily be rude. That way, when he is, I'm not shocked and then he can't manipulate me as easily." Her lack of shock kept her in an emotionally level state that then allowed her to proceed with logic, not false guilt or intimidation, guiding her moves.

Humility Sees Assertiveness as Responsible

In chapter four, we explored how people pleasers, with the history of suppressing anger, have a need to choose assertiveness more often. Let's take that thought one step farther. Would you consider it an act of pride to refuse to be assertive? Your initial reaction might be, "I can see how nonassertiveness implies fear, but pride? Carter, where did you come up with that?"

Keep in mind that pride prompts individuals to be preoccupied with selfish motives whereas humility promotes a mindset that considers all persons involved in a situation, not just self. When you refuse to be assertive in situations where it is warranted, you are so busy protecting yourself that you are failing to factor in the good that can come from being open about your convictions or your needs.

You may protest, however, and say, "But nothing good comes when I'm assertive. The other person only becomes more difficult." Again, that could represent self-absorbed thinking, as if it is too inconvenient for you to do something that might be uncomfortable. Also, you may be assuming that in your assertiveness it is your job (which it is not) to make the other person agree with you or change in order to create a cooperative atmosphere.

Indeed, something good *does* come from assertiveness even when the other person is not pleased with what you are communicating. Take Eilene, for instance, the woman who endured condescending treatment from her husband for years before they separated. By holding in her convictions, was she being a servant? Was she being a helpful participant in the relationship? Not at all. While on the surface she was kind and dutiful and compliant, in the end she was so engaged in self-protective behavior that she brought harm upon herself *and* her husband, Walt.

When I first mentioned this to her, she questioned how her compliance would harm Walt since he so pompously lorded over her in smug self-satisfaction. I explained, "I think you'll agree that the way he treated you was often wrong. I'm sure you registered protests from time to time, but when all was said and done, he knew not to take you seriously. By withholding assertiveness, you quietly communicated, 'Go ahead and treat me poorly because I'll take it.' It seems strange to say that pride was a factor in that thinking because it seems so self-effacing. Indeed, you were so entrapped by your own short-term considerations that you could not recognize how you were passively contributing to a very unhealthy system.

"In humility," I continued, "you would remind yourself that it's appropriate to look out for others' best interests even as you also take care of your own. Sometimes that humility could cause you to think, 'Even if he wants to act irresponsibly toward me, I cannot in good conscience participate.'"

Eilene thought very carefully for a moment, and then asked, "But what about the church's instruction that I'm supposed to be submissive and that I should regard my husband above myself?"

I was familiar with the passages in Ephesians, chapter five, and Philippians, chapter two, that instructed a considerate, submissive spirit. "I'm not about to argue against the wisdom of Scripture," I replied. "In fact, I take it to be the blueprint for a healthy lifestyle. What I'm saying is that sometimes *in an act of submission* you will say, 'No, that is not a godly way for me to live.' In humility you will stand for what is pure and godly, and you will not go along with someone else's unhealthy requirements."

Her eyes growing larger, Eilene replied, "I must say, I've never thought about it from the angle you're presenting. This is a *very* different slant on the subject of humility."

A humble (or submissive) person is committed to the things that are best for a relationship, even if it sometimes cuts against the conventional thinking. So let's not assume that humility is parallel to "doormat-ism." Humility is the source of inner strength, the kind that prompts individuals to stand for what is pure rather than to cower in self-protection.

Consider that Christ was the embodiment of humility, yet there were numerous times when he would use assertiveness. For example:

- When the disciples wanted to chase away young children who had been brought by their mothers to meet Jesus, he felt indignant toward the disciples and reversed their action. (Mark 10:13–16)
- When Jesus had an opportunity to heal a man with a withered hand on the Sabbath, the Pharisees disapproved. Feeling both grief and anger, Jesus healed the man anyway, much to the Pharisees' dismay. (Mark 3:1–6)
- Despite the grumbling of some people in Jericho, Jesus invited the hated Zacchaeus to lunch. He was not going to alter his behavior to appease critics. (Luke 19:1–7)

Many times Christ would press forward in assertiveness to accomplish a goal, knowing that others would not approve. Even as he maintained a mind of humility, he also displayed strength, choosing to stay the course that was part of his personal mission. Can you think in a similar fashion?

Be aware, as Eilene was, that others may not appreciate the view of humility that actually encourages you to stand firmly for what you know is best. "You're being controlling" may be their protest. Or you may hear, "This is not at all a spirit of cooperation." When you hear such protests, be willing to take a hard inward look to determine if indeed your motives are self-centered. If you honestly know that you are holding firm to necessary boundaries, then proceed firmly yet non-abrasively.

To further illustrate how humility can be demonstrated in the midst of firmness, consider the following adjustments made by Eilene and Anita:

- Once Ted told Anita he thought it was unfair to ask him to adjust his Saturday golf schedule to accommodate needs she had in getting their girls to different places. Anita knew she was valid in her request so she stood firmly without engaging in an unnecessary argument.

- Eilene learned that when her sister made a request for her time, she could say, "That sounds valid, so I'll help you. Now, could I ask you to help in kind by recognizing my need to keep the activity limited to an hour?"

- Anita knew that her father was easily irritated when she handled child discipline different than he would. She decided she'd stick to her convictions, yet she would display a kind and patient spirit toward her dad, knowing he would always be "old school."

- When Eilene would learn that Walt was still saying unflattering things about her behind her back, she would gently tell the person caught in the middle that her perspective was quite different, yet she would bypass the opportunity to speak ill of Walt in response.

I recall as I spoke with both Anita and Eilene about establishing themselves as servants without a prideful foundation, each realized how honesty required them to admit that there was more of a self-pleasing aspect to their people-pleasing behavior than they had ever admitted. Are you willing to acknowledge the same? When you get out of the mode of self-preoccupied thinking, perhaps you can recognize that others actually *need* the good perspective you bring to the table. They may not *like* it, but you can certainly attempt to communicate those perspectives in the most appropriate way possible.

In the next three chapters, we will explore more fully how you can move toward a way of life that is still pleasing, but not in a self-defeating manner. In the next chapter, we will explore how you can make the necessary changes by claiming a trait that has probably been woefully lacking in your life: freedom.

For Personal Reflection

When you think of a prideful person, what stereotyped image usually comes to mind?

_____

_____

_____

What might be some of the blatant forms of pride that you see in others?

_____

_____

_____

How about you? What forms of pride are most common in you?

_____

_____

_____

How would you define humility? In what ways could this trait be shown in your life?

_____

_____

_____

When do you need to communicate more clearly that you are a person who needs to live within reasonable limits?

_____

_____

_____

_____

When do you indulge the thought: "I deserve" or "You owe me"?

_____

_____

_____

_____

How would your emotions level off if you dropped your notions of deservedness?

_____

_____

_____

_____

In what ways might you demonstrate humility by being assertive?

_____

_____

_____

_____

Section Three

Finding Balance in Your Life

Chapter 8

Choosing Freedom as a Way of Life

Duty. Obligation. Indebtedness. Restriction. Subservience. These are words that could describe a life that overemphasizes people pleasing. Most people in this pattern will very quickly point out that they are connected with key people who are controlling or blaming or moody. Not wanting to make matters any worse than they already are, people pleasers will acquiesce to the overbearing ways of the more overpowering persons, assuming that they have little option but to try not to make waves. When this happens, a feeling of powerlessness results. The people pleasers then feel ensnared by their unpleasant circumstances, as they tell themselves that they are just destined to live under someone else's dominance.

I spoke with a woman, Annette, whose first words to me captured the essence of the powerlessness felt by people pleasers. "I feel as if I'm everyone's slave," she began. "From the minute I get up to the time I go to bed at night, I'm jumping through someone's hoops." Just five or six years out of college, Annette had taken on the adult world by storm. Vivacious and easy with a smile, she told me she had been specifically taught that trouble makers never made it to the top. Only the ones who learn how to blend into an organization can expect to make it. No one likes the grumpy know-it-all who would push aside his own grandmother to get a few steps ahead. Now, in her second corporate job in the pharmaceutical industry, she was experiencing major burnout, and she was also questioning the choice she had made for marriage.

Annette had always been very conscientious about treating people fairly, but the reason she sought counseling was due to increasing temper outbursts as well as occasional anxiety spells. The week before seeing me she had been rushed to the hospital with severe chest pains, thinking she was having some form of heart failure. "Stress reaction" is what the doctor diagnosed. "That's when I knew I had to seek help," Annette told me. "Something's getting way out of hand."

I asked her to talk with me about those stressors, and she had no trouble identifying several. "My life is definitely not playing out as I would have liked," Annette said. She spoke with the intensity of the well-trained marketing rep that she was. "I've got a boss who is absolutely unreasonable in her expectations of me. I'm a pretty organized person. I have to be because I've got a crowded schedule most days; but this supervisor of mine has no qualms about making me totally rearrange my schedule at the last minute, and most of the time she has really stupid reasoning for what she asks me to do. I work with doctor's offices and pharmacies, and it's a very competitive world out there. I can't afford to be yanked around by someone as capricious as she is because I don't want to look foolish to the people I call on."

She then proceeded to tell me more about the agitation produced by people who stood her up for appointments or made promises that they clearly knew they wouldn't keep. Then suddenly she shifted gears as she began talking about her four-year marriage to Shane, a man she had met through friends. "You know, I wouldn't mind my work so much if I knew I was going home to someone who really appreciated me," Annette said, "but that's just not the way it is. Shane says he loves me, but I swear I couldn't tell by his actions. He's got a demanding job, too, so you'd think he would know how necessary a supportive home life should be. Instead of being someone understanding, he has all these mood swings that make him impossible to predict. I never know what kind of husband is going to walk through the door at the end of the day. Sometimes he's friendly as he can be, but usually that just means he wants sex. Other times he's real grouchy and nothing will please him. Sometimes I get a call at the last minute when he's telling me he'll be late so he can go to a ball game with a buddy. Of course, he never checks to see if it interferes with my needs; he just announces what he's going to do, and then he does it." Red blotches covered Annette's neck as she spoke.

"I can tell this all wears you down. Can I assume that you have ongoing conflict with your supervisor and with your husband?"

"Well, I guess if I was normal you could assume that, but that's really not the case. Maybe I need to be more of an in-your-face con-fronter, but that's just the problem—I'm not! In fact, I disgust myself because I'm so compliant. Instead of saying anything about these problems, I'm afraid of swatting the bee hive and creating a swarm. Both my supervisor and Shane can have a temper, or at least they can get really edgy. So like a robot, I just go along with their whims and let them walk all over me."

Annette had two major problems in the situations she was describ-ing. First, she had genuinely difficult relations with two controlling people; second, and most significant, she did not see herself as a per-son possessing the freedom to make the wisest choices in these mat-ters. To get an idea if you too can relate to the problem of feeling confined in your relationships, put a check by the statements that would frequently describe you:

_____ 1. I have learned that I shouldn't think or feel too differently.

_____ 2. I get the sense that I'm supposed to stay in the mold others have defined for me.

_____ 3. I dare not say what I really feel, knowing it would create too much friction.

_____ 4. If I ever do try to explain my perspective, it's likely to be met with invalidation.

_____ 5. Too much of my time is spent appeasing someone else's moodiness.

_____ 6. In my world, it's not okay to make mistakes.

_____ 7. Many of my decisions are based not on my own preferences, but on the preferences of others.

_____ 8. My priorities too frequently are determined by someone else's demands.

_____ 9. When I complete a project, I know it's going to be criticized or heavily scrutinized.

_____ 10. Sometimes I will alter my own good judgment just to keep the peace with others.

It is common to feel, at times, that you are under the influence of a controlling person, so it would be unusual if you related to none of the statements. If you checked five or more, you are likely to feel controlled much of the time. You probably hesitate to express your uniqueness because you know it will be met by a person's putting clamps on you.

The Necessity of Freedom

A cornerstone characteristic in both healthy personalities and relationships is freedom. We Americans love to celebrate the concept of freedom—so much so that we have a national holiday which reminds us of the fact that our country's founders built this nation upon the bedrock of freedom. We cheer when we hear the news of a dictatorial governmental regime being toppled, and we react with scorn when we hear news of a despot's controlling hand over the masses. We cling to the belief that freedom is given to humanity by God and it is the responsibility of governments to preserve that freedom.

Do we have the same high regard for freedom in our marital relations or at work or in our discipline of children? Sad to say, many individuals who think highly of freedom on a large, global scale cannot bring themselves to allow freedoms on a relationship level. Most of the people pleasers I counsel can tell tales of having to determine how they can best get along with persons who have a strong controlling bent, who will refuse to recognize personal freedoms. Using words like "supposed to" and "have to" and "should" and "must," these controlling people make it their business to fit people into the mold they believe to be best. The people pleasers, wary of engaging in battles they are sure to lose, give up their freedoms as they attempt to appease the controllers. The net result is depression, discouragement, anxiety, futility, and the like. My goal is to help these people realize they are doing no one any favors by giving up their freedom, the privilege to choose who they will be.

As I got to know Annette, I talked with her about the need to claim her freedoms. "You seem to have at least two key people in your life who want to deny you the privilege to choose how you will conduct your life. You seem to be driven by a long list of 'can'ts' and 'musts' and 'got tos'."

Shaking her head, she said, "That's the way it is in my life: one long agenda that spells out for me how I'd better live. No one seems to ask my opinion about what I think is best, but I'm just told what to do and I do it." Then emphatically she added, "And I *hate* it."

"Well, let's see if you'd be willing to shift gears in the way you approach the agendas that others have for you," I responded. "Let's first affirm that God has placed in your personality a free will, and it is your prerogative to use that will any time and in any way you see fit. How does that sound?"

Thinking for a moment, she finally reflected, "I *think* it sounds okay, but I'm not sure. I mean, it's hard to argue against the idea of freedom, but don't you think that could be risky? I could see that this would lead to a problem of chaos and irresponsibility if it's taken too far."

"You're right. It *could* lead to irresponsibility since there is always the possibility that you could choose to use your freedom poorly. Freedom is not without risk." Then to add perspective, I reminded her, "When freedom is denied, that is the first step toward enslavement, and I don't think that's something you'd want willingly to agree to."

When I talk with people like Annette, I want them to understand that any personality does not function well when it is placed under the yoke of another person's control. To make wise choices, we need to know first that we are not under compulsion to do what we do. Giving her a simple illustration of what I meant, I said to Annette, "Suppose I had just completed a conversation with you and I had stepped down the hallway to talk with a colleague of mine. This colleague mentions that he noticed how I spent time with you, so he asks me how our conversations are going. My response is: 'Well, you know that the Bible says I'm supposed to be kind to people, so while I was talking to her I acted kindly; I did what I had to do.' How would you feel if you overheard me saying that about you?"

Chuckling at the absurdity of the illustration, she replied, "Well, you know I wouldn't like it one bit. I'd be hurt and highly offended."

Making my point I said, "Strangely enough, my choice to be kind would be devoid of its meaning if I was acting out of sheer duty. Only when I know that I have the freedom to be unkind would my kindness have any real appeal." Then continuing, I mentioned, "Too often you do what others expect of you, but only because you feel obligated. When sheer obligation is your motivation, your behavior may appear correct on the outside, but inwardly you are not acting upon a well-conceived free choice, and that feeds emotional tension."

Annette began recalling one incident after another in which she did what she had to do even though it did not ultimately concur with what her free will would have led to. For instance:

- She constantly altered her schedule for Shane "just to keep him off my case."
- She was very guarded in talking with her husband about the events of her day because she felt she had to dodge his inevitable critical remarks.
- She begrudgingly went along with him to social outings with his friends, whose moral character was suspect at best.
- When she talked with her father about her financial circumstances, she would give him the answers he wanted, even if they weren't completely accurate.
- With friends, she would agree to help with projects that she had neither the time nor interest to do well.

On and on she went in citing situations in which she acted as if she was enslaved by other persons' demands.

Can you relate? Do you recognize that when you go too far into your people-pleasing behavior you can ignore the reality of your God-given freedom, opting instead to place yourself into a type of bondage that is not good? (Lest we take our thinking too far in the other direction, let me affirm that service and self-denial are good traits when they are chosen for the right reasons. People pleasers, however, may act serving but do so because of fear or false guilt).

Think for a moment about the way your life could be different as you allowed yourself to do what you do because you freely chose to do so. What would change? That's the question I asked Annette, and it prompted some major soul-searching.

"You know, I like the idea of freedom because it helps me realize that ultimately I'm responsible for who I am. This might seem odd to you, but I've never really put a lot of thought about what a free me would look like."

"One good thing can come from your struggle to incorporate a free mindset. It can cause you to grapple deeply with the issue of who you really are. Up until now, you've let others' commands determine who you'll be, but I'm encouraging you to go before God and decide with His help what your identity will be. The results might be quite different."

The Hidden Messages of Control versus the Hidden Messages of Freedom

To understand more fully why control is a far less successful orientation than freedom, let's examine some of the covert messages that accompany each mindset. By covert messages I mean that each communication transaction between persons can have a strong yet unspoken implication that shapes the way the transaction affects the individuals involved. As you become aware of the covert signals that shape your emotional disposition, you can make better informed determinations regarding the ways you will conduct yourself in your relationships.

Non-acceptance versus Acceptance

When a controlling agenda is present in a relationship, acceptance is absent. As people place controlling requirements upon you, they are simultaneously insinuating that you do not make the grade in your current status. The *overt* message of the controlling person may be quite good or correct. For instance, a controlling person may say, "You've got to be considerate of my time constraints," or "You should be willing to tend to my legitimate needs." Often it is hard to argue against the logic of the controlling person's outer message. Yet despite the seeming correctness of what is being said, there is usually an unspoken implication: "I cannot and will not accept you in your current status. Meet my correct conditions and then we'll talk about acceptance, but not until then."

While it is impossible for fallible humans to demonstrate pure unconditional acceptance, that is a lofty goal worthy of aspiration. Certainly each of us has beliefs about morality or values or just common sense that we hold to. It is good and necessary to stake out what you believe and prefer. Yet it is not good when those beliefs and preferences become barriers to a loving attitude. To illustrate, I recall a man who once confessed to me, "I'm so right that I'm wrong." He went on to explain that along with his mind of correctness came criticism and abrasiveness and rejection toward others. He confessed that as he craved control more and more, he was able to love less and less.

When people engage with one another, whether it is in the context of family or work or friendships, a key ingredient that makes that relationship thrive is acceptance. This does not mean that you have to let go of the convictions that mean the most to you. It does mean, though, that you place a higher priority on love. Controlling people have a hard time giving love the higher priority, and unfortunately, people pleasers (often driven by an unhealthy denial of what they know to be best) will comply with the controlling person's demands even though they know it will result in their feeling unloved.

When I counsel with people pleasers, I emphasize that they may never be able to change the non-accepting attitudes of controllers, yet they are not required to play along with its unhealthy aspects. I told Annette, "I think it's unfortunate that Shane takes it upon himself to tell you what to do even when it's unreasonable and when it creates an atmosphere of non-acceptance. It sure would be nice if he'd change, but at this point, I guess we can't count on that." Continuing, I said,

"Even if he does not accept you in your free state, that doesn't take away the reality that you are nonetheless free. If you act against your will, you are actually embracing the assumption that your uniqueness is indeed unacceptable, and I don't think that's really the way you want to think about yourself."

"I never really thought about it that way," Annette replied, "but now that you explain it that way, it's as clear as day. So where do I go from here?"

"Let's recognize that when you agree with the fact that you are a free person, you are simultaneously confirming the truth that you get to accept yourself as you are. You don't have to fit someone's mold to find acceptance, nor do you have to read their minds first. You have permission to be what you are, even as you are different or imperfect."

Can you think that way? Like Annette, many people pleasers will need to reconsider some of the powerful lessons learned during their developmental years which emphasized the need to perform for acceptance. It will be necessary to recognize the fact that self-acceptance can be claimed even when performances do not meet others' standards. For instance, in freedom Annette chose to:

- Accept the fact that she didn't have to cater to all of Shane's scheduling demands. It was acceptable to follow her own priorities.
- Drop her guard when talking about her day as she realized that Shane's moodiness did not make her perspectives any less appropriate.
- Determine for herself if it was desirable or not to go on social outings which involved people whose character was less than desirable.
- Talk with her father about her finances only as she felt it appropriate, realizing she had the intelligence to decide the best way to handle her own matters.
- Say no to friends' requests that did not fit her priorities, and accept the fact that it was good for her to establish her own uniqueness.

Like Annette, you can choose to maintain self-affirming beliefs even in the midst of your differences with others. In doing so, you are also choosing to separate yourself from the restrictive conditions that controlling people would wish to impose upon you.

Non-trust versus Trustworthiness

Just as acceptance is absent in the communication from a controlling person, so is trust. While the controller may not openly state, "I don't trust you," the message is strongly implied. When trust is present in a relationship, there is no need to be forceful or manipulative because it is assumed that the other person will receive the input fairly based on its merits. Openness and optimism, then, are common ingredients in the communication. When communication has a strong demanding or judgmental aspect, however, the communicator is sending a clear signal that assumes that the receiver is likely to act in an untrustworthy manner if allowed the freedom to respond in an unrestrained fashion.

As an example, Annette told me of an incident in which Shane complained about his sister's finicky ways. The two of them were going to visit Sis on a Friday evening, so Shane took it upon himself to instruct Annette about the ways she should behave in her presence. "He was telling me what subjects I could talk about and what I couldn't. He tried to tell me what to wear. He told me how long we were going to stay at her house and how I was supposed to act toward her little son. I mean, he had this long list of do's and don'ts, and he was going to make sure I complied with everything he said."

"How did that affect you?"

"Not good at all! He must think I'm some sort of moron who is incapable of thinking for myself. It's like he can't trust me to use a little common sense around his sister."

He can't trust me. While Shane did not actually speak those words, that's the message clearly received by Annette. Shane may have been accurate in everything he said to Annette, yet his method of communication portrayed such little confidence in her ability to think for herself that the legitimate portions of his communication were lost. Whether it was a conscious thought on Shane's part or not, his controlling manner was so laced with a lack of trust that Annette was hardly able to hear anything but that.

Now let's take this problem a little farther. Many people pleasers, while not liking the implication of non-trust, will think to themselves, *Well, even though my intelligence and trustworthiness are not respected, I guess I'll comply because I don't want to make waves.* They will then become appeasers, and in the process they prop up the very attitude in the other person that they strongly dislike. They might as well say to the controller, "Go ahead and distrust my capabilities; you're probably right in your assessment of me."

"Wow! Is that the message my compliant behavior sends?" Annette asked. "Most of the time Shane barks his orders at me, and I just go along to get along, but I wasn't aware that I was encouraging him to hold to a non-trusting view of me." Then she asked, "What other options do I have?"

"First, let me reinforce the notion that I like it when you are willing to be cooperative. I'm not going to suggest that you turn into a combative rebel every time he speaks to you with non-trust. What I am saying, though, is that you can try to educate him regarding your own trust in yourself. You can let him know that you'll receive his input, but you reserve the prerogative to choose for yourself how you will act."

"I'm not sure he'll like that. Shane's very opinionated and if I talk back, he'll go straight into an argumentative mode, and one thing's for sure: I can't out-debate him."

"The good news, Annette, is that you don't have to out-debate him. You don't have to offer any grand rationalizations for your decisions either. Let him think whatever he wants. Remember, you're free to be what you are and he's free to be what he is, too. I'm simply suggesting that you calmly display that despite his lack of trust in you, you trust in yourself. You're not obliged to comply or to defend yourself. Just let him know, with no unnecessary justification, that you'll handle matters as you see fit."

Just a few days after our conversation, Annette and Shane were getting ready for a social outing when Shane began instructing her just as he had done prior to going to his sister's house. This time Annette handled things differently. "Shane," she began, "I know it's important to you that I handle myself well when we're with other people, so that's something I'm already tuned into. I like the way I manage my relationships and right now I'm not really needing any guidance." When Shane tried to continue with his unsolicited advice, she gently touched his shoulder and said, "It's OK. I'm going to be fine."

Later Annette told me, "I was consciously aware that I needed to let him know that I trusted my own abilities, so much so that I didn't have to cower to his overwhelming ways, but I also didn't have to convince him of my virtues. It was different for me, but it felt good."

As you claim your freedom, you can also stand firm in the belief that you can be trusted to handle most circumstances reasonably. You are not beyond the need for instruction or enlightenment, yet you are indeed a person whose values are reasonable. As you embrace such thinking, you will sidestep the need to prove your trustworthiness by complying with demands that you may not believe are really necessary. Instead you can proceed with your own good judgments, and if that is not pleasing to the controllers in your life, you can reckon that it is their responsibility to come to terms with their control problem, but it is not yours to solve or placate.

Inferiority versus Equality

When your freedom is ignored and control is over-used, another implied message is one of inferiority. Specifically, the controller is insinuating to the compliant appeaser, "I'm superior to you, and don't you forget it." It is as though the controllers have weighed the value of their opinions or preferences versus those of the other person and they have declared themselves to be of higher stock. While not spoken, their behavior sends the signal, "Sorry, you're beneath me."

Despite the obvious insult that accompanies controlling behaviors, people pleasers often find themselves going along with the message of devaluation. By not acting freely, but living under the burden of over-compliance, people pleasers are quietly suggesting, "Go ahead and think of me as inferior; I'll probably agree with you."

I spoke frankly with Annette about her tendency to accept inferiority as an inevitability in her relationship with her husband. "When you come in here, I see an energetic young woman who has a lot of talent and very reasonable people skills. Your capabilities and your value are certainly on par with anyone. The baffling thing about you is that despite your strengths, you'll accept a position of inferiority when someone appears to be of a stronger opinion than you. Has this been going on a long time?"

"Well, first, you're right. I guess it *is* baffling that I would buy into a low opinion of myself, because the truth is I *am* a decent, capable person. And yes, this has been going on a long time—too long, I'm afraid. I remember as a girl being afraid to be too different because it was frowned on by both of my parents. They were very strict and they always had a good rationale for their beliefs, so even when I disagreed with them, I realized it would do no good to cut against the grain."

What I heard from Annette was very similar to what I had heard numerous times from other people pleasers. While children need a measured amount of freedom to act upon their own beliefs, most people pleasers recall that their childhood years lacked the privilege to choose, but instead was typified by strong commands or expectations to conform with little regard for reasonable uniqueness. As a result, they did not learn to believe as fully as they should about the adequacy of their own reasoning ability. They may have developed a rebellious feeling, yet they still felt it necessary to comply because of the assumption that in the end their notions were probably not legitimate.

Notice what can happen when people pleasers accept the position of inferiority:

- You can apologize for things that need no apology.
- You have good ideas that you don't pursue because someone might scorn them.
- Self-doubt can dominate your decision-making processes.
- You go along with plans that you disagree with.
- You won't hold your ground when someone wrongly argues with you.
- When you are confronted in a disagreement, you will make unnecessary concessions.

- You might tell someone you agree with him even when you don't.

To change, you will need to recognize the inappropriateness of the superior-to-inferior form of communication. You can become motivated to respond to controllers in a manner that is more consistent with the mind of freedom. That is, you can relate with would-be controllers as one equal to another. You can recognize that while indeed there can be moments when others have more forceful opinions, that does not have to be interpreted as superiority. Instead, you can assume that your perspectives carry just as much value as anyone else's . . . and you are not required to "prove" the validity of your thoughts. (That's the *free* part.)

As I spoke with Annette about allowing herself the freedom to relate as an equal to anyone, she realized she had to make some major thought adjustments that would then lead to behavior adjustments. For instance, she recognized:

- There was no need to apologize unnecessarily. She could let her sound judgments stand on their own with no defense.
- She could act upon her own good notions as opposed to filtering them through others' potential reactions. Why? Because her thinking was on par with anyone's.
- She would stick to a decision without going through agonizing self-questioning.
- Knowing her instincts were good, she could choose when to go along with others' plans and when not to.
- When others argued unfairly with her, she could calmly state, "I'm standing on my convictions." No further arguments.
- Just because someone confronted her, she did not have to make immediate concessions. She could state, "I'd like to think it over."
- She would not state that she agreed with something she disagreed with.

In freedom, you will not accept the position of inferiority, nor will you attempt to turn the tables by acting superior. You can recognize that God made personalities different, *yet equal,* because He prefers it that way. Your differentness can be understood as having nothing to do with inferior or superior status.

Think for a moment about your life. In what circumstances could you afford to claim more freedom? If controlling persons attempt to deny you that freedom, can you recognize that it is not their position either to give or take freedoms, but that you possess freedom as a God-given privilege?

As you claim the freedom to be you, you can still choose to be a pleasing person, but let it be for the right reasons.

For Personal Reflection

To you, what does it mean to be free?

_____

_____

_____

_____

In what ways do others attempt to deny you the privilege of choice?

_____

_____

_____

_____

In what ways do you voluntarily accept an unhealthy yoke of subservience?

_____

_____

_____

_____

How would your relational style change for the better if you chose more consistently to accept yourself as you are?

_____

_____

_____

_____

In what circumstances could you afford to operate with more self-trust?

_____

_____

_____

_____

How can you best respond if others have difficulty accepting the reality that you are free to make your own choices?

_____

_____

_____

_____

If you determined to relate with others as one equal to another, how might this result in improved relations?

_____

_____

_____

_____

Chapter 9

Maintaining Ongoing Assertiveness

In chapter seven, you were challenged to recognize that your people pleasing can sometimes have hidden, prideful motives. That is not a pleasant thought, but your willingness to tackle it marks a major step forward. In this chapter, we will operate with the realization that others also have moments when they get caught in their own prideful traps.

In addition to the pleasing contributions to a relationship, then, it is necessary to have a game plan to help you confront the "dark side" that is part of other people. Sad to say, each relationship can have its share of misunderstandings, manipulation, selfishness, arguments, coercion, withdrawal, and the like. It's not a very pretty picture to contemplate, yet it is an inescapable certainty: people can and will disappoint.

Because a defining element of the people-pleasing pattern is the avoidance of conflict, people pleasers can acknowledge with their minds that frustrations and aggravations will be an inevitability, yet they often will not acknowledge through their behavior that they are ready and willing to properly guard themselves from the pain produced in conflict. Firmness, assertiveness, can be a necessary ingredient in any close relationship, yet people pleasers will often do anything but act assertively, and the results can be disastrous.

As I got to know Tommy, the computer whiz introduced in chapter two, I realized that he would almost rather take a beating than stand up to someone else's selfish behavior. Being a nice guy was such an important matter to him that he had numerous circumstances where he went along with unfair treatment to avoid conflict. Internally, he struggled with ongoing bouts of bitterness and he secretly disliked many of the people he helped, yet no one would know it because of his winsome smile and his seemingly pleasant demeanor.

One day Tommy began a session by declaring, "I absolutely hate where I'm working. I don't know what the deal is with my manager, but he puts expectations on me that no one else has to perform. He's got me putting out so many fires for other people that I feel like I'm being pulled in ninety different directions. Everyone else in my section leaves the office around five or five-thirty every day, but last week I didn't get home once before eight o'clock. There's a double standard going on and I'm on the short end of the deal."

"Sounds like you've got a good reason to feel upset. Is this something you've talked with your manager about?"

"Yeah, about five months ago in my employee review we talked about the fact that he leans on me in ways that he does with no one else. He knows he can count on me to pull through in any crisis, which is both a blessing and a curse. I told him then I wished he didn't have quite so much confidence in me and we both laughed about it."

"Was anything decided in that meeting that would help you feel less burdened?"

"Well, nothing formal. He *did* mention that he knew I had a lot on my plate and he'd try to spread out the assignments a little more evenly, but at the same time, he told me he often had no one else to turn to because I could figure things out so much more efficiently than anyone else. The extra requests slowed down for a few weeks, but as you can tell, I'm back in the same pot of stew now."

In chapter four, we discussed how people pleasers have a strong tendency to suppress their anger. When they do so, they bypass many opportunities to establish assertiveness in their major relationships.

Like Tommy, they may make feeble efforts to confront their problems, but in the end there is little firmness, meaning that other people feel free to continue to take advantage of their helpful nature. Until these people learn to follow through on their assertions, it is likely they will continue to feel used.

Assertiveness can be communicated in various ways. Look over the following list to determine which forms of assertiveness you need to improve upon. Place a check by the statements that represent an area in need of improvement.

_____   1.   You can speak firmly about matters of importance while simultaneously giving respect.

_____   2.   When someone attempts to engage in unnecessary debate, you can let it be known that you'll explain your position once but you won't defend.

_____   3.   You can address problems in an immediate manner, as opposed to letting them simmer.

_____   4.   You will say "no" when that is the appropriate response.

_____   5.   You can let people know what you can and cannot do. You will set boundaries.

_____   6.   Admitting personal limits is something you will do when you're asked to do something that is out of your range of capability.

_____   7.   You will do what is right, even in the midst of opposition.

_____   8.   You can stand firmly for your beliefs.

_____   9.   You can choose not to buckle under the pressure others may put on you.

_____   10.   You are not reluctant to let people know how they can help you address personal needs.

There are moments for each of us when we could be more assertive, so if some of these statements look like areas for improvement, that is normal. If you checked five or more, it is likely that assertiveness is a skill you need to work on, but don't despair. With a solid understanding of its appropriateness, you can make the adjustments!

I spoke with Tommy about the problem of feeling overwhelmed by the extra requests placed on him by his manager. "Whether you realize it or not, you send cues to others, telling them about your limits in the relationship. I'm concerned that it has become so important for you to project a friendly image that you cue others to believe they can take advantage of you. By learning when to establish boundaries or stipulations you could cue others to take your personal limits more seriously. It's up to you to establish how you'll be treated."

"I know I need to do a better job of saying no, but I just don't think it will be that easy. I've truly been helpful to my coworkers and it will probably shock them if I start denying some requests. I know I'll encounter resistance."

"First of all, Tommy, don't assume that changing your relational style should be easy. You've been at your people pleasing your entire life, so it will feel odd at first to take on a new role. At the same time, though, I'm going to guess that not everyone will be shocked when you establish some assertiveness. I'd bet that many already notice that you take on too many projects and they're just wondering when you're going to tell them to back off."

"You nailed it there," Tommy replied. "I've heard over and over from people who say they are astonished at the load I carry. So maybe you're right. Maybe I *could* afford to be a little less like Superman and admit to anyone who needs to know that I'm human."

The Components of Assertiveness

As Tommy and I discussed ways his assertiveness would be established, several adjustments emerged as we explored his options:

1. He did not need to say yes to every request for help from his coworkers.

2. When his priorities differed from his extended family's, it would be OK to allow that differentness to stand as long as he knew he was remaining responsible and moral.

3. When his wife invalidated his perceptions, he could nonetheless hold firm and calmly state, "I'm going to stick with my good instincts."

4. Knowing he wanted more balance in time spent at home in the evenings, he chose not to stay at the office beyond six o'clock.

5.   As he sensed frustration building in his relations with family and coworkers, he realized it would be good to talk about it rather than suppress it as he had done in years past.

These changes and many more helped Tommy become a more well-rounded person, and in the end, his pleasing behavior seemed more real and rewarding. Let's examine together how he came to terms with his newfound commitment to assertiveness, and as we do, you too can consider how your thinking and your behavior can be changed to bring a similar balance into your life.

As you ponder the ways you need to apply more assertiveness in your life, keep in mind that assertion is an act of responsibility. In the long run, you're doing no one any favors by taking more onto your shoulders than is reasonable. Assertiveness is not always comfortable, nor is it always readily received by those who are affected by it. Nonetheless, you will need to consider the long-term benefits of being more honest, more real in your relations. Keep in mind that as assertiveness is properly balanced in a relationship, it clears the way for the greater possibility of love and consideration. Also remember that if assertiveness causes a relationship to wane, it probably was not a healthy relationship to begin with. By choosing assertiveness, you are choosing healthiness, something that is not experienced when you become excessively compliant.

In order to make assertiveness a more natural aspect of your relating style, it would be helpful to recognize four of its key components.

#1. Open Recognition of Differentness

My home's backyard is not what you would call a botanical garden, but we enjoy growing a wide variety of shrubs, herbs, and flowers. With the changing seasons, we try to determine what new plant life we will grow, and we enjoy the beauty of crepe myrtles, begonias, impatiens, hydrangeas, sedums, zenias, tulips, lilies, Texas bluebells, mums, and many other plants. What makes us appreciate our garden so much is the incredible variety of colors and shapes these plants represent. Certainly we would be disappointed if every plant looked the same and grew at the same time. Variety is what we celebrate!

While it is easy to sing the praises of the variety found in nature, many people are not quite as enthusiastic in embracing the variety found in human personalities. On the surface, perhaps, people will say it is good to experience differing personal perspectives, but when perspectives become too different, many people will automatically become persuasive as they attempt to create conformity and sameness of mind. Have you ever encountered people whose goal was to rid you of your personality's uniqueness?

That was a problem that Tommy encountered often. "You know, it seems that any time I indicate that I'm on a different wavelength from others, someone feels slighted by that, and then they set out to whip me into the groove they want me to be in." He spoke with great exasperation in his voice. "Just last weekend I was about to leave the house to take my son out to a field to fly a remote-controlled model airplane we had built. This is a hobby I really enjoy, and it gives me and my son something to do together because he enjoys it every bit as much as I do. Before we left, I got a phone call from my mother, and when I told her what we were about to do, she instantly went into a questioning mode. She asked me why I had to spend so much money on something frivolous. And she said it didn't make sense that my daughter couldn't go along with us because she would enjoy that type of outing."

"Sounds like it just took the zip right out of your Saturday," I commented.

"Well, yeah, it did! Then I got to thinking that she's talked that way to me my entire life. Any time I wanted to take a different path, I knew I'd first have to endure her lectures or questions. It got to the point that I didn't want to expose anything unique about myself because I'd have to explain why it was OK for me to be me."

"Have you had similar experiences in other relations as well?"

"Yes. It seems like there are a lot of people who don't want me to be different. And what's worse, I have a history of caving in when someone questions why I might want to do something out of the box."

Does this sound familiar? Commonly, people pleasers have been trained to think that it is not good to be too different, that it is their job to learn the expected norms and conform. In the meantime, they suppress the aspects of their personality that are unique to them, often feeling shame or guilt for things that are not wrong or immoral or unethical. For instance, was it wrong for Tommy to fly model airplanes? According to his mother it was, but to Tommy it was not. In fact, it was great fun and provided a means to bond with his son.

When you embrace the mind of assertiveness, you can begin by allowing yourself to be unique, no apologies required. Tommy was different from his mother, and it was necessary for him to act upon his differentness with a full resolve that he was doing at that moment what he needed to do. He needed to be true to himself.

Think about the many ways you could establish assertiveness by holding firmly to your uniqueness. For instance:

- In a discussion, when it is clear that you hold a perspective that the other person does not, stand firmly on your beliefs. It is acceptable to have this differentness.
- When you react to a situation with a different emotion, you do not have to quickly rein in that emotion. Be open about what you feel.
- If someone tells you he disagrees with the way you handled a situation, but you know you handled it well, respectfully hear him out, then stick to your plans.
- When a person speaks coercively to you about changing your mind, *without defending yourself* you can say, "I'm comfortable with my decision."
- As you tell others about personal beliefs, you are not required to soft-pedal just because you know the other person believes differently. Be who you are.

While assertiveness is not the same as being stubborn or dogmatic, it is typified by the firm realization that your differentness is not an occasion to cower. You have feelings or needs or desires or preferences that others do not have, and that in itself is not grounds for rejection or judgment. If others choose to reject or judge you, nonetheless, you can still permit yourself to be uniquely you. To do otherwise would be an invitation to greater emotional duress.

I explained to Tommy, "I'm assuming that you're ultimately not very good at being something that you're not. In the short term, you can fool people into thinking that you concur with them, but as you falsely portray yourself in too strong of a conformist pattern, your bitterness or hidden rebellion will be an indicator that you've pushed yourself too far. By using assertiveness, you are letting your behavior reflect the higher notion that it is indeed OK to be you. Your differentness is not bad; it's just . . . well, different."

In what circumstances do you need to openly embrace your uniqueness? You may find that others may not know exactly what to do with your uniqueness, but as you show that your uniqueness is accompanied by fair-mindedness and respectfulness, perhaps they will figure it out. Openly celebrate the fact that you are not the same as all others.

#2. Establishing Ownership of Your Mission

Once you embrace the validity of your uniqueness, you can take your thought life to a higher plane. No longer will you be required to conform to standards that do not fit. Instead, you can anchor yourself in a mission designed specifically for yourself. This means you will take on priorities that are within your scheme of what you believe you should be.

In chapter five you were encouraged to ponder your purpose or mission in life. This requires contemplation about serious issues of spiritual matters, beginning with questions about God, the meaning of life, and your definition of success. However, it can also include contemplation about more minor matters such as how you will let your day's schedule unfold, how you will conduct yourself in social surroundings, or how you will budget your money. All these matters are part of your purpose, and no one can ultimately define those things for you except you.

People pleasers, however, will report that there may be many people who will attempt to establish your mission for you, as if that is their prerogative. Tommy, for instance, told me that he enjoyed his work, and it was his belief that he should pursue a career in a way that utilized his skills while also providing a means to support his family. It sounded good to me. But, he added, he had people at work who seemed intent on revising his personal mission. Though it was not stated, they implied through their demands for extra time that his personal life did not need to be given the high priority that Tommy felt it should.

"When I'm at work late into the evening, taking care of someone else's dilemma, I get the feeling that my life is being defined for me by someone else, and that just doesn't seem right," he explained.

"Not only is it not right," I commented, "but I doubt that those people made the effort to learn how their requests fit into your beliefs about who you should be." We both chuckled as we realized how absurdly true my statement was.

As you practice assertiveness, you will need to stick to your vision of how your current circumstances fit into your overall definition of who you are. For example, if Tommy were asked to stay late for a meeting that would interfere with valuable family time, it would be good for him to excuse himself, explaining he had other things in his schedule needing his attention. On a lighter note, if his wife wanted him to do extra chores while he had planned on a couple of hours of needed leisure, he could tell her that in order to be most effective he needed the downtime he had carved out for himself. Tommy could maintain peace of mind in these situations once he genuinely knew his decisions were based on reasonably considered ideas that fit into his overall mission to be a balanced man.

"You know, Les, when we sit here in your office discussing this, it seems reasonable just to hold firmly to my beliefs that might take me onto a path where others don't particularly want me to go. But when I actually try to act it out, it still feels odd, like maybe I'm being disloyal or I'm cheating somebody."

To live outside your life's mission is irresponsible. Your gestures of assertiveness are an indication that you believe in being true to your purpose even if it means that you will have moments of disagreement or discomfort. Taking on this attitude, though, may indeed feel odd at first, but let's assume that you can get used to it!

#3. The Need for Directness

People pleasers tend to have an uncanny knack for creating positive impressions in situations when they do not feel positively, and that is not good. How many times, for instance, have you been asked, "How's everything going?" and you replied, "It's going fine," when in fact things really were not fine? Over and over I hear people confide how they really feel a great amount of hurt or anger or disgust, but they will not let it be known.

There is nothing heroic about covering up unpleasant emotions. While you may assume you can give an impression that satisfies the person in front of you, that is a short-sighted way of living. Over the course of time, your real self will find a way to surface, no matter how hard you try to please by giving a false impression.

By committing to assertiveness, you are recognizing that open and direct communication is far more desirable (and ultimately successful) than coy communication which is intended to deflect short-term discomfort. Direct communication adds a much needed element of honesty to your relationships, and it establishes you as one who is trustworthy.

Annette, the energetic young woman who burned herself out trying to please her husband, had pushed herself to fit properly as a new wife. The result was depression for her while her husband interacted with her with little awareness of how she really felt. "Annette, I'm wanting you to live with the best ingredients leading the way in your relationships," I told her. "For you to have the marriage you want, it would be best for you to shoot straight with your husband. For Shane to blend with you, he needs to know what you really feel and think."

"I'm not sure that can be done," she replied. "I've tried to tell him on numerous occasions how I feel, and he doesn't seem to hear it. In fact, he can be pretty argumentative. That's when I just give up and do whatever it takes to keep peace."

"I'm all for peace," I said, "so let's not assume that the alternative is war. I suspect you spend too much time defending yourself when he dislikes what you say, and since you can't out-debate him, you then back down from your convictions."

"You're exactly right. Sometimes I can't get a word in edge-wise because Shane can be so forceful."

"When I suggest that you be direct, I'm not saying you should take it upon yourself to make him agree with you. You don't have to become an in-your-face combatant. Say what you need to say, hold firmly to your boundaries, and when he tries to draw you into a senseless debate, let him know you're going to remain firm but you are not going to try to convince him to endorse what you are saying. By being direct, you can be what you are without having to retreat into a mode of rationalizing or even apologizing for what you choose to do."

"Boy, that would be different," was Annette's reply. "That would mean that I'd project a much stronger backbone than I have before."

It was Jesus himself who said, "Let your yes mean yes and your no mean no." It is not good to waffle in your communications when it means you cannot be trusted to be a person whose internals are consistent with the externals. Consider some of the ways you might be able to be direct in appropriate ways:

- When asked to do something that clearly does not fit your priorities, you can explain succinctly that you are going to expend your energies elsewhere.
- When your children don't want to do as you ask, rather than pleading with them to obey, you can calmly explain the consequences for their choices, then follow through as needed.
- As a friend tries to entice you to agree with a position that seems out of line, you can politely yet firmly state that you hold other ideas.
- If a coworker seems to request more attention than seems appropriate, you can let her know that you have other priorities requiring your attention.
- If an extended family member puts guilt on you for choosing a separate priority, you can communicate that you feel right about your decision, and then proceed.

As I spoke with Annette about having more directness in her communications, she remarked, "You know, it makes good sense to do as you suggest, but I'm not sure I can do this very well in real life. I live with a pretty strong-willed man."

"When you've got a deep history of appeasement," I replied, "directness can be unnatural at first, particularly as you realize others may be taken aback by it. In order to succeed, you will need to see directness as a choice, not a requirement. You can choose to continue suppressing your convictions and live with the consequences, or you can choose to be true to who you are. Personally, I think you'll feel cleaner as you choose the latter."

Direct communications show that you believe in your decision-making capabilities, that you know you deserve respect. Excessive people pleasing can communicate the opposite. While being direct, you can still be respectful to others, and in the meantime you are upholding a sense of dignity for yourself.

#4. Refraining from Unnecessary Defensiveness

Often people pleasers will make a good first attempt to be assertive only to realize that their reasoning is quickly invalidated. Immediately, then, these folks will lose their resolve and retreat into a defensive mode. At that point, the other party can smugly assume, "Well, I put you in your place by showing you who's boss."

Let's ponder a very basic question. Why defend something that needs no defense? Most people pleasers will protest to me by saying something like, "I don't know why others put me on the defensive, because I'm not *that* offensive of a person!" My reply is, "If you're truly in the right, then stand upon your correctness without defending it."

As an example, Tommy told me about a discussion he'd had with his eleven-year-old daughter, Mary. "I told her last weekend that she couldn't spend the night with a friend because we had too much to do the next day. She started whining, which made me feel like I had to explain my position more clearly. Before you know it, I was bargaining with her, offering her enticements so she'd go along with my restriction. Is that a case of the inmates running the asylum or what?"

"Why were you so quick to give in to her complaints? Sounds to me like you made a reasonable decision that she could learn to live with."

"I don't know, but I do that kind of thing constantly. I can be open about what I think is best but as soon as someone second-guesses me or suggests that I'm wrong, I go into this mode where I try to show that I'm really a good guy, not some mean jerk."

"It sounds to me like you can't let yourself believe you're a good guy until you receive the full agreement of that person in front of you."

Does this sound familiar? Do you retreat into a defensive posture too readily when you need to stick to your convictions? As you commit to clean assertiveness, you'll realize that excessive defensiveness is unnecessary. A general rule of thumb could be: Explain your reasoning once; then if you are invited to defend what needs no defense, don't.

When you act assertively, you are attempting to stand firmly for what you know is right or best while also being considerate toward the needs of the other person involved. However, there is a catch. There is no assurance that the other person will receive your assertion as valid. It is at this point that you have to make a quick determination. Is that person's invalidation of you a reflection of your incompetence or is it perhaps a reflection of that person's unwillingness to receive legitimate input? Too often people pleasers will assume it is their own personality at fault rather than realizing that others may be imposing their own close-mindedness onto the interaction.

I try to explain to people like Tommy and Annette that they are doing no one any favors by jumping quickly into a communication of rationalizing or justifying. Rarely are their defenses met with agreement or appreciation. Instead, as they go deeper into defensiveness, they are virtually inviting others to think less of them. By not defending, these people may not succeed in getting others to understand their reasoning, but they *do* succeed in the sense that they stand firmly on their own merits.

Tommy reflected carefully on that thought. He said, "You know, I've always known that my thinking is as sound as anyone else's. Maybe I'm not right every time, but I'm reasonable in my logic and in my priorities. It makes no sense then that I will so quickly succumb to someone else's opinions, particularly when I know that my convictions can be trusted."

I reflected, "It seems to me that you would be better off as you say what needs to be said or do what needs to be done, and if others want to take shots at you, that's their prerogative, but you're under no obligation to have to enter into tit-for-tat discussions." I asked him to make a list of common scenarios where he could speak convictions more freely, defending less powerfully. Here's a sample of what he wrote:

- When my mother attempts to maneuver my schedule, I'll recognize that's my job to handle, not hers, even if she doesn't understand my reasoning.
- When my kids question the validity of my decisions, I'll explain to them once why I've decided as I have, and then I'm finished with my end of the discussion.
- If my coworker doesn't like the fact that I can't drop what I'm doing to work on his problem, then it's not my place to make him understand that I have my own work to do.
- When I feel like relaxing and my wife is doing some housecleaning, there's no need for me to convince her that it really is OK for me to want some rest.

"Can you stick to these positions that you wrote?" I asked him.

Smiling, Tommy said, "I'm going to have to if I'm planning on keeping my sanity. I've spent so much energy for years trying to plead my case to people who didn't want to hear my perspective that it's time for me to face reality. If I can stand before God and know that my deliberations are reasonable, then I guess it's not necessary for me to go off and try to get human approval." Pausing for a moment, he then added, "It'll be a new behavior, that's for sure."

As you try to replace the habit of defensiveness with a new habit of calm assertiveness, it may indeed feel unnatural. Natural or easy feelings, though, do not need to be your primary concern. Doing what you know is healthy—that should be foremost on your mind. Assertiveness may never be something you enjoy, but make sure you are committed to being the best you need to be in your relations. That includes openness and appropriate honesty.

In the next chapter, we will examine how you can strengthen your resolve to be assertive as you determine how to respond to some common objections you may run into.

For Personal Reflection

What does assertiveness mean to you?

_____

_____

_____

_____

In what ways could you afford to be more assertive?

_____

_____

_____

_____

In what ways could you accept more openly your own differentness from others?

_____

_____

_____

_____

What could be your response when others communicate that they do not like your differentness?

_____

_____

_____

_____

_____

In what circumstances do you find directness to be awkward?

_____

_____

_____

_____

How would your relationships improve if you learned to be more appropriately direct?

_____

_____

_____

_____

When do you defend yourself unnecessarily?

_____

_____

_____

_____

In what ways might others feel empowered when it is obvious that you are too defensive?

_____

_____

_____

_____

Chapter 10

Responding to Objections to Your Assertiveness

Virtually all people pleasers know they are not in for a smooth ride when they determine to opt out of the excessively compliant role. In fact, that is typically what keeps these people bound to the pattern of deferring to others' stronger or more persistent demands. "I don't want to have to hassle with the objections I know I'm guaranteed to receive . . . it's just not worth it!"

When I talk with these people about making the needed adjustments, I may use an analogy of a person's trying to lose twenty pounds. To lose weight, you will need to exercise in ways that you know are good for you, even though you'll probably ache for the first several days. In addition, you will need to eat and drink what is right and refrain from those things that are not good. Self-restraint and discipline are not always easy, nor do they always feel good, but they can still be the best options.

To sustain your motivation, remember that there are long-term positive results that you can glean:

- Your relationships will not be clouded by "unfinished business" caused by avoidant communication.
- You can be free from hidden bitterness or resentment.
- Your communication will become far more honest and genuine.

150

- You will be acting upon your own beliefs, not the beliefs imposed on you by others.
- You may at times encourage others to take responsibility for their own lives, as opposed to letting them put that burden on you.
- You can become known for having a calm, confident demeanor.
- Others can recognize that you are deserving of respect.
- You will rightly recognize that you have limits and you can't do it all.

One sure thing you will need to brace for is the objections you will receive when you communicate your limits and assertions. Some of the objections will be sent in the form of direct rejection. Sometimes you will be "invited" to debate. Other times, you will be ridiculed. (I'm being honest here. It may not be an entirely pretty picture.) So you may ask, "Why bother?" The answer is that the alternative to healthy interaction is ever-increasing ineffectiveness at life skills. People pleasers learn, sometimes through painful lessons, that what they attempt to do to minimize problems only increases their problems.

So, are you ready to move forward? If so, you will need to arm yourself with some balanced thinking as you prepare to respond confidently to some predictable objections. I posed this question to Richard, the real estate developer who had gotten himself into a bind between his wife, Alecia, and a female coworker, Karen. "You know, it seems so out of character for me to avoid conflict because I've always been known as someone who could deal head-to-head with any circumstance. Right now, though, it seems that I'm not in the mood to deal with the conflict if I begin being totally straight with either Karen or Alecia. You might say that I've become a pain avoider."

"Actually, the better term would be *pain postponer*," I remarked. "As you remain in the excessive people-pleaser pattern, you are only increasing your chances for misery. The pain you are attempting to avoid will only be worse as you play dodging games."

Richard knew I was right, so he had to take a hard personal inventory to determine if he was ready to face the possible protests to his balanced assertiveness. Before we examined what he might encounter,

I had him check to determine if he was mentally prepared to face the challenge. You too can do the same by reading the following list. Put a check by the statements that can apply to you.

_____ 1. I can see that firmness on my part is long overdue. It is a quality I need more of.

_____ 2. My convictions are generally sound, to the point of being trustworthy.

_____ 3. Too much of my emotional energy is spent trying to make others happy. That needs to change.

_____ 4. I'm ready to admit that if others are overbearing, it may be their problem to solve, not mine.

_____ 5. Even if others interpret me wrongly, I need to proceed with my best determinations.

_____ 6. I know that I can continue to be thoughtful even as I am also more decisive.

_____ 7. I have a purpose for my life that I'm determined to pursue.

_____ 8. It is necessary for me to voice my opinions and preferences, not because I want to be pushy, but because I have good things to offer.

_____ 9. When others try to entice me to live outside my boundaries, I can see that I'm being responsible to stick to my convictions.

_____ 10. I consider openness or genuineness as a quality that I am very committed to.

Hopefully, you can place a check next to each of the above statements. As you realize that you have good reasons to act in ways that are most consistent with your values, you can still be a pleasing person without also having to let others dictate your decisions. If you could only check five or fewer, I would encourage you to rethink the appropriateness of firmness and assertiveness. It is likely that you are still selling your own good virtues short.

Common Objections

As you prepare for a life of more self-assured decisions, realize that others may still cling to their own self-focused thinking. This means that they may attempt to invalidate your good efforts by putting you back onto a path of false guilt. Don't let that happen! In order to stay steady in your efforts to be assertive, let's examine several common misconceptions you may hear regarding assertiveness. As you can conceive in advance your response to those misconceptions, you can sustain the strength to stay above the problem of unhealthy people pleasing.

#1. "Assertiveness Implies a Rebellious Spirit"

One of the major reasons you may over-emphasize people pleasing is that you are exposed to demanding people who have preconceived notions regarding the way you are supposed to behave. These people have a mold you are supposed to fit, and there is a great price you have to pay when you stray. When you succumb to such an overwhelming atmosphere, you are concurring that indeed your priorities are not to be trusted, meaning compliance to others' demands is mandatory.

As you choose to follow your assertiveness, however, you are endorsing your legitimacy. That is both good and necessary. Unfortunately, the demanding people in your life may not have the same interpretation. Wanting to shame you into going back to the mold, they may say, "You're acting like a rebel." They will then shake their heads as they try to figure out how to make you give up your independence.

As an example, Richard told me that part of his burnout had been set up by years of being everyone's "go-to guy." In any organization, he eventually assumed a leadership role because people had great confidence in his decision-making skills, and he assumed it was his duty to please. He would take on more commitments than necessary; then he would quietly feel frustrated because he had too many people vying for his time. By the time he had made friends with the business associate, Karen, he had decided to scale back greatly on his outside commitments, and people were wondering what was wrong with him.

Richard told me about an incident at church. "A guy pulled me aside last week and asked me to run interference for him with an attorney he was working with regarding a parachurch organization they were putting together. Apparently, there was a snag in their proceedings, so this man assumed I was just the guy to go to the attorney and iron it out. Sure enough, I knew the attorney; but the problem was not one that I knew anything about, so I told him I wasn't the right person."

My response was, "Sounds like you were making a reasonable judgment, particularly if someone else might have been more appropriate to handle the problem."

"That's exactly what I thought, but this guy kept pressing the point, so I calmly held my ground. I really did keep my cool. Later on, though, I learned that he was bad-mouthing me, saying that I used to be loyal to church matters but now he was questioning my cooperative spirit. I was being labeled a rebel just for saying what was right!"

Has this ever happened to you? Are your separate preferences ever interpreted as rebellious or disloyal or disobedient? If you haven't had that experience yet, realize it is a very real possibility. How would you respond to such a false accusation?

By saying no, Richard was exercising his free will. Often, people are fearful of allowing you to be free because it is possible to use freedom irresponsibly. We all have known people who have declared themselves free from others' controlling clutches only to run with that freedom in the wrong direction. When you exercise free will, others may be drawing upon experiences with someone other than you who did not handle freedom well. That is unfortunate, but *you are not required to accept a false label.*

I told Richard, "I suppose if you went years, or even months, turning all requests down, we might be able to make a case regarding a rebellion problem, but this is just one incident. Let that man at church have whatever opinion he wants to have, knowing that in time the ongoing strength of your character can still be seen. In the meantime, sidestep his mispronouncement."

With all his might, Richard had to resist the temptation to take on the request the man had asked him about, but he realized he didn't have to prove himself. No longer relying so heavily on public approval for his security, he knew he was not a rebel, so that could be enough.

#2. "Assertiveness Means You're Selfish"

Some people go a step beyond the accusation of rebellion as they conclude that your assertiveness is proof that you are a self-absorbed machine. Using an all-or-nothing mindset, they assume that if you are not willing to set aside a desire or priority, then it means that you have no team spirit at all. They presume that all needs should be placed above your own.

Very often, the persons accusing you of selfishness may actually be the ones suffering from that problem. They are so consumed with their own agendas that they can see no further than the end of their own noses. However, not wanting to admit that their preferences are selfish, they use a defense mechanism known as projection, ascribing to you what they do not want to admit in themselves. People pleasers are often so worried about being seen as selfish that they do not always recognize the hidden agenda behind the false accusations.

As I talked with Richard about finding balance in his life of people pulling on him, I explained, "True assertiveness is never selfish. Yes, it does prompt you to take actions to address your own needs, but it is done only as you know that you are factoring in the needs of the other people involved. As you realize you are not being cruel or insensitive in living out your assertions, you can proceed with calm confidence. Now, it may be that the other person is lazy or manipulative, meaning your assertiveness may not be well received, but it does not necessitate your going into a waffling mode."

Realize that true assertiveness is anchored in self-preservation, which is not at all the same as selfishness. Every day you do small things to preserve your legitimate needs. You bathe yourself; you eat; you get some sleep; you enjoy a little leisure activity. These things are good, and as long as you can fit them around your daily responsibilities, you are not under a selfish label. In the same way, you need to care for your basic emotional needs by saying no or setting stipulations or delegating chores. You can do this, *not* because you are selfish, but because you want to keep yourself operating at peak effectiveness. Running on overload is not the way to remain effective.

Richard reflected, "You know, it's disillusioning to know that people have leaned on me for so many years, and now that I'm pulling back in order to gain my personal bearings, I'm thought of by some as selfish. It makes me wonder if the people I thought were my friends really are friends at all."

He was experiencing a common aftereffect of people who have rightly chosen to be a little less enabling. "You may not be wrong to interpret others' protests as a reflection of their own selfishness not yours. I think the building struggle over the years with burnout indicates that you were out of balance, so your partial retreat is actually needed. If anything, your people-pleasing behavior had become so extreme, *that* was the selfish behavior because it indicated that you had become too consumed with your approval from others." Assertiveness brought balance, not self-absorption, to Richard's life. Despite others' accusations, could you see assertiveness as a trait that ultimately makes you *more* capable of being a true servant? It can be your way of saying to the world, "When you interact with me, expect balance, not imbalance."

#3. "Assertiveness and Submission Are Incompatible"

When I speak to Christians about healthy assertiveness I will often field a question about submission: "Doesn't the Bible say women are supposed to be submissive to their husbands?" My answer is, "Yes, so what's the problem?" The reply can be, "Well, it sounds to me that women could take your teaching and turn it into license for a non-submissive spirit." My reply is, "That could happen, but it is not my intent." Then I very quickly point out that the Bible is equally clear for husbands to be submissive, as well as citizens and children and church members and people in leadership.

Too many people assume submission requires people to comply with "superiors" even if that compliance feeds wrong behavior. That is not submission; that is enablement, and it is not healthy in either a spiritual or a relational sense. Submission means that any individual, in whatever role they act, will seek out God's will to be the most appropriate and helpful person they can be in that role. Many times submission results in acts of kindness and service, things that leave others feeling good. Other times, submission will lead persons to say no or to draw lines of resistance, not because they are mean-spirited, but because they are committed to being people of character and integrity.

A submissive husband, for instance, whose wife treats people rudely will tell her it is his intent to follow the path that he knows is more loving. She may accuse him of being non-cooperative, but that does not make him so. A submissive wife may choose to spend time with a friend against her husband's wishes, not because she's trying to find ways to irritate her husband, but because she is doing good in the relationship with the friend without detracting from family responsibilities. His judgmental demands do not mean she must shut down her decision-making skills and do everything his way. That would not reflect submission, but enslavement.

Annette, the twenty-something pharmaceutical employee, told me, "Shane and I have a lot to learn about submission. Virtually any time I try to pursue a different preference from his, he tells me I'm not submissive. Because I don't want that label on me, I'll often back down. Just last weekend, I told a girlfriend I couldn't spend a Saturday afternoon helping her pick out curtains because Shane wanted me home. He had golfing plans for that morning and didn't want to come home to an empty apartment. We didn't even have plans, but I felt like I had to do what he wanted because I'm supposed to be submissive."

"Annette, submission is a mutual quality. It is a trait for each of you to use equally. Yes, it's good for you to factor in his schedule as you plan yours, and it is also good for Shane to do the same in reverse. As marriage partners, you need time together, but it can also be legitimate to have other outside support relationships. Submission is not an all-or-nothing proposition that requires you to check your brain at the back door."

When you act upon assertiveness, ask yourself first: Do I have a good pattern of cooperation already established? Am I being reasonable in my assertion? Is the protest against my choice due to love or due to control needs? As you are convinced that you are a servant who is considerate in establishing your priorities, proceed in the awareness that when someone accuses you of non-submission, that does not necessarily reflect reasonable or considerate thinking.

Sometimes assertiveness is the most submissive choice you can make. For instance, if a husband speaks to his wife in egotistical, insulting ways, her commitment to being a godly woman could prompt her to say she cannot agree to his unloving demands. Her motive is not selfish, but it is anchored in a commitment to uphold her God-given dignity. Taking such an approach may feel out of character for chronic people pleasers, yet it can cause them to realize that fearful subservience is a poor substitute for a commitment to a healthy life.

#4. "Being Assertive Is the Same as Declaring War"

When you have a combination of imperfect people, whether in the home or at work or at church or in friendships, conflict is inevitable. Over time, the imperfections will surface, as will simple differences in priorities or beliefs. That is no particular cause for alarm. Healthy relationships make room to openly discuss conflicts without resorting to judgments or coercion. These relationships actually want their members to be assertive so there will be the least chance for the buildup of tension or misperceptions.

Unhealthy relationships, however, do not allow for open discussions about conflict. They can operate with the unspoken rule that assumes you are an unruly or troublesome person if you are open about disagreements. Anchored in egotistical cravings for control, these folks might say, "If you express differences, you are asking for a fight." Then they feel justified in using "warfare tactics" based on your "uncooperativeness."

For instance, Annette told me, "My first year of marriage to Shane was awful. The minute I'd express a frustration or hurt, he'd accuse me of being impossible to live with. As I'd examine my communication, I could honestly say that I was careful in what I said and how I said it, but in Shane's mind, I was just trying to pick a fight. Part of my appeasing behavior stemmed from my desire not to be thought of as a combative person."

Can you relate to Annette's situation? While it is good for you to consider the possibility that you should be careful and judicious in addressing conflicts, it is also good for you to remain committed to a reasonable discussion of differences. In fact, in healthy relationships, the participants actually can celebrate the presence of differentness. Recognizing the value of diversity, these people can still find ways to harmonize by *openly embracing* the need for perspectives that stretch the mind.

To underscore this reality, you need look no further than First Corinthians, chapter 12, where Paul addresses the issue of the diversity of gifts within that church's community. Not only does he not equate differentness with increased conflict, he teaches them to have a high regard for the varieties of skills and perspectives among the people.

I told Annette, "I hope Shane can eventually get to the point where he not only accommodates your uniqueness, but that he actually appreciates it. In the meantime, if he wrongly accuses you of being a troublemaker, it will be necessary for you to have enough confidence in yourself that you're not inhibited by false accusations. You don't have to hold to your convictions with a spirit of defiance. Instead, calmly let him know that you feel right about your perspectives and you will always be open to hearing his."

"That's not going to be easy, because any time I talk like that, he becomes argumentative. It's not my style just to stand firm knowing he's mad."

Sympathizing with that predicament, I responded, "I'm hoping that over the course of time, your calm resolve, accompanied by your ongoing cooperative spirit, will demonstrate to him that you are not using your assertiveness to be an adversarial figure."

As an example, on another Saturday, Shane again announced that he would be playing golf in the morning and he expected Annette to be home when he finished. She gently told him, "I've got a lot of errands to run, so I may be a little later getting home than you." When he went into his predictable pout, Annette put her hand on his shoulder and explained, "I'm really looking forward to spending the rest of the day with you once we get our other matters out of the way. Don't worry, we'll have a good afternoon and evening together." As she held her ground, she was establishing that she was not his adversary. She was merely doing what a normal wife would do on a Saturday. While she couldn't guarantee that Shane's protests would immediately die down, she determined that her goal was to be a balanced, loving person as opposed to being a beaten-down, ineffective foe.

#5. "Assertiveness Signals That You Have an Anger Problem"

If you have a deep history of excessive people pleasing, you have probably unwittingly "trained" others to think of you in less than respectful ways. By being over-willing to set aside your own legitimate needs, others have been allowed to assume that you are not one to be taken seriously. As an example, Annette told me that Shane came from a very male-dominant home where he and his dad had a different standard than his mother and two sisters. "When he ran out of tea at the dinner table, all he had to do was shake the ice in his empty glass and one of the females would get up and pour him more tea. He learned that it was acceptable to feel superior to them."

"When you first learned this about him," I asked, "how did it affect you?"

"Oh, I protested, all right! I told him not to expect the same from me, but you have to know Shane . . . he's such a smooth operator. With his kidding smile and his playfulness he can charm anyone, and before you know it, he had me doing similar things." With her voice taking a more serious tone, Annette added, "In the last several weeks, I've been explaining to Shane that I still want to be a servant, but not at the expense of my self-respect, and not as a one-way street. I've told him that it's fair for me to ask him to help with some of the tradition-ally female chores, you know, like vacuuming or cleaning the kitchen. When he tries to escape, I don't let him off the hook like I used to. One of these days, we'll have kids and I want my children to see women treated with respect, so I figured we need to start that trend now."

"That's different from your old self-effacing style," I commented. "So how's he handling it?"

"Not real well. He tells me that I've got an anger problem."

"Well, do you?"

"I told him that I *would* have an anger problem if I continued in my non-assertiveness. Honestly, as I talk with him about my needs, I'm concentrating on having an even tone of voice and a non-combative spirit, just like we've discussed, but he's not used to that. He's really struggling to figure the new me out."

Did Annette have an anger problem? Based on her description, no. The problem was not in her emotional management, but in Shane's insensitivity. Annette needed to be wise enough to consider the possibility that she could go overboard in her new-found assertiveness, yet as she was confident that she was "speaking truth in love" (see Eph. 4:15), she could sidestep his erroneously directed protest.

Assertiveness is not a problem as long as you know that your subject matter is valid and your method of delivery is respectful. If someone complains that you are being unfair, be willing to consider their needs; but then if you still reckon yourself to be appropriate, hold firmly without apologizing.

#6. "Assertiveness Means You're Burning Bridges"

More than a few times I've heard stories from formerly excessive people pleasers whose adjustments led to some serious breakdowns in relationships. For instance, do you remember how Tommy complained because his mother expected him to plan every holiday and every special event around her? Tommy slowly began to recognize that she was selfish because of the dogmatic nature of her desires and because of the emotional fits she would have if he hinted at alternative plans. (Remember, this is a man in his forties.) So he began giving himself permission to make plans outside her preferences . . . but he learned that she could make matters uncomfortable.

After not spending an entire four-day Thanksgiving weekend with her (he stayed overnight), she refused his invitation to celebrate

Christmas with him at his home. "She was mad, so this was her way of punishing me," he explained.

"So what happened next?"

"I didn't take her bait and I think it shocked her. In the past, I would have run through fire to make her happy, but this time I decided she could have her pout and it wasn't my place to appease her. I didn't hear from her until Valentine's Day, and she wasn't happy. She accused me of burning bridges in our relationship."

What do you think? Was Tommy burning bridges? No. With his history of pacifying her excessive demands, he was finally doing what should have been done twenty years earlier.

He did hear her make that complaint, but in this case, it was the mother burning bridges. By her withdrawal, she was communicating, "You do things on my terms or I'll cut you off."

Though sometimes assertiveness may result in relationships going in new directions, that is not the same as cutting yourself off from the other person. By definition, assertiveness represents a commitment to the things that are right and best. When you are assertive, you are extending yourself to be a contributor to a win-win exchange. If the relationship deteriorates as a result, it is usually symptomatic of the other person's ongoing refusal to embrace goodness. In being assertive, your goal should never be the absolute dissolution of a relationship. If however, the other person chooses to pull away, you should not necessarily be held prisoner if it means you will be required to accommodate their selfish desires.

As Tommy and I discussed the implications of his firmness with his mother, I explained, "I *want* you and your mother to enjoy the years you have left together. So even as you draw your reasonable boundaries, I'm also hopeful that you will continue initiating good interactions."

"That's my plan. I'm going to let her know that I can't continue being intimidated by her tantrums, but I'm also going to include her in my life. This isn't the all-or-nothing ordeal she's fearful it would be." I knew then that Tommy was coming to a solid sense of balance in his family life.

#7. "Your Assertiveness Causes Pain in Others"

As a parent, I have had numerous situations through the years when I have had to draw a line that did not elicit a wonderful reaction. I can recall moments in my daughter's toddler years (she's now sixteen) when I'd tell her she couldn't do something she'd asked to do, and so she would cry. Did she feel pain? *She* thought she was in pain. Was I a sadist inflicting the pain? Well, that was a different story. As a responsible parent, I would maintain solid convictions that occasionally created a moaning reaction, but it would be too far of a stretch to say that I was causing pain. I was only telling her something she didn't want to hear.

The same can be true in adult-to-adult relationships. You can be direct or assertive and the other person can clearly feel pain, but that does not mean you are an agent of wrong. The pain could just as easily be caused by the other person's unrealistic expectations.

Annette had a very serious discussion with her husband, Shane. "First, I want to tell you that I love you and I'm committed for life to you," she began. "You've noticed that I've been making some adjustments and I'm not as willing as I used to be to play an inferior role. You have my assurance that I will be here to serve you and do all I can to make your life good. At the same time, I'm not going to choose to go along with condescending treatment." As she spoke, Annette was calm with gentleness in her voice.

She told me about this conversation and as I asked about his response, she said, "Well, it was interesting. For the first time ever he had tears in his eyes and he told me he couldn't talk then, so we spent the rest of the evening not talking. The next day, he told me he'd lain awake most of the night thinking. He'd known prior to my bringing attention to it that he'd not been very sensitive to me, and it had been getting worse. He felt a lot of disgust toward himself and vowed that he'd be making some major efforts to turn the tide."

Did Shane feel pain? Yes. Did Annette cause it? No, she brought him to an awareness of it, and in doing so, she helped him make adjustments for the better.

As you consider the assertive alternatives to excessive people pleasing, remember that your goal is to improve the overall nature of the relationship. When you go too deep into a mode of compliance, *that* can be the unhealthy contribution. The frustrated reaction by others as you change styles can be likened to a child's growing pain. The people mentioned in the illustrations typify how it is not always easy to redirect relationships that are founded upon poor habits. Committing to godly, fair interactions may not be fun while the adjustments are put into place, but the final results can be quite rewarding.

In the next chapter, we will examine the possibility that some people will continue to be intrusive despite your efforts to bring about needed changes. Do you know how best to respond? Stay tuned.

For Personal Reflection

In what ways are your life skills increasingly ineffective when you continue to buckle under others' overpowering ways?

_____

_____

_____

_____

How does assertiveness differ from rebelliousness or an uncooperative spirit?

_____

_____

_____

_____

When might others be prone to interpret your assertiveness as selfish?

_____

_____

_____

_____

In what ways can your assertiveness actually indicate a commitment to true submission?

_____

_____

_____

_____

How might assertiveness redefine some of your key relationships?

_____

_____

_____

_____

What hurt might someone else feel when you are assertive?

_____

_____

_____

_____

How can you know if that hurt is caused by you or if it is caused by the other person's own demanding nature?

_____

_____

_____

_____

Chapter 11

Dealing with Intrusive People

For years, Jean had felt torn because she could not figure out how to handle her mother. It's not that the mother was an unlikeable woman. To the contrary, she was friendly and fun, and you would hardly ever meet anyone with a bigger heart. She gave to Jean and her husband of ten years, Steve, in many ways. Living just ten minutes away, the mother was a great grandma. She loved Jean and Steve's seven-year-old son, Seth, dearly and was readily available when Jean needed her to assist in his care. Jean knew she could call on Mother, for instance, if she had to visit a doctor or if she needed someone to pick up Seth after school. She was truly willing to do whatever she could to make life as pleasant as possible for her daughter and grandson.

So why was Jean torn? Steve and Mother were not close, and for good reasons. Through the years, Mother had been so eager to fill her role as grandma that she often overstepped her boundaries. She was the kind of person who didn't listen well. She wouldn't take no for an answer. So if Mother called to say she was going to drop by for a brief visit (which was rarely brief), Jean might tell her it wasn't a good time, but in a few minutes, she'd show up at their house anyway. During the first few years of their marriage, Steve had not protested too much about Mother's over-eagerness to be in their lives, but as time had passed, Steve had become more vocal about his feelings.

"Why is it that we can't have a peaceful Friday evening at home without your mother having to cook up something for us to do? I'm not saying I don't want her in our lives, but I would like to have a little distance. I'll bet Seth feels like he has three parents. She's *so* available that I feel crowded!"

Jean knew Steve to be a balanced man in his emotions, not one to grumble readily. If he was complaining about something, it probably had merit. For instance, one Saturday morning, Mother had called, excited because she'd just had a new tile floor laid in her kitchen. "You've got to come see it. I'm so pleased with the way it turned out." As Jean hung up the phone to tell Steve they'd need to run by Mother's house, Steve commented, "Don't you remember? I told Allen that I'd meet him at the driving range in about thirty minutes. You'll have to go without me."

"Oh honey, can't you just drop by Mother's house for a few minutes? She's all excited and wants to show off her new floor. You don't want her to be disappointed, do you?"

"That's not the point. I'm not going over there because I've already made plans; and besides, it's not like it'll be months before I have a chance to run by and see it."

Jean knew Steve was right. He didn't *have* to go to Mother's right away, but she dreaded telling her mom that Steve had other plans. Predictably, she would say, "What do you mean he went to the driving range? Is that so important the he couldn't come here for just a few minutes?" Mother was a master guilt-inducer. She was kind and giving, *but* it came with a price. She expected loyalty (translated: obligation to do what I want you to do) and she readily pouted or complained when she didn't receive it.

All her life, Jean had felt compelled to please her mother. She had been the type who had made all of Jean's childhood friends feel welcome in her home. She had been home-room mom at school. She'd directed her in children's choir at church. She'd sacrificed a career in interior design so she could spend time with Jean and her older sister,

Kate. Now at age thirty-three, Jean felt Mother was constantly calling in her favors. "I've done so many things to help you," went Mother's reasoning, "that surely you could spend a little time with me." Most of the time, Jean was able to comply, but increasingly Steve resented feeling intruded upon by her. Jean didn't necessarily disagree with Steve for wanting a little distance. Sometimes she wanted it too. What paralyzed her was the indecision regarding the best way to handle Mother, knowing she wouldn't handle her assertions with acceptance.

Can you relate to Jean's plight? Most people pleasers project an attitude of willingness or cooperation only to find that some people misconstrue that as permission to be overly involved in advice-giving or in prioritizing their lives. Because people pleasers can be reluctant to be assertive and set healthy boundaries, patterns can emerge whereby they feel overwhelmed by the intrusive person who just can't see the imbalance in their behavior.

Maybe you are like Jean in that you feel intruded upon by a parent or a member of the extended family who wants and needs you to the point of over-involvement. Perhaps you have kids whose high maintenance needs overwhelm you. It could be that your employer wants more from you than you can give. Maybe you have over-committed yourself at church because of people who won't take no for an answer. It could be that you have friends or even a spouse who is too needy, to the point of being clingy.

It is good that you would want to be available to people in times of need. Loyalty and charity are noble traits for you to maintain consistently. In the meantime, though, you can feel pushed to the point of emotional overload if you do not choose to set appropriate stipulations in those relationships that can become stifling.

To get an idea if you are under the burden of having to deal with an intrusive person, place a check by each of the following statements that would apply to you:

_____ 1. There are people in my world who won't accept no for an answer.

_____ 2. When I try to establish a boundary, others seem ready to talk me out of it.

_____   3.   I have been made to feel guilty for things that are not wrong.

_____   4.   There are people in my life who seem to think I'm more necessary to them than I really am.

_____   5.   My desire for separateness is too often interpreted as selfish or uncooperative.

_____   6.   There are some people who just won't take the time to consider my perspectives.

_____   7.   I have to tread lightly so I won't hurt someone's feelings or make them angry.

_____   8.   When I give, it seems others just want more.

_____   9.   I receive advice or directives from others even when I don't need it.

_____   10.   I often feel like I am under the burden of others' expectations.

It would be normal if you could respond to some of these items since we each can have exposure to others' expectations or demands. If you checked five or more, it is possible that you have intrusive people in your life who will continue to be that way if you don't learn to establish your uniqueness. The more you cater to them, the more likely you will feel burdened by unneeded stress.

One reason you may hesitate to be firm with intrusive people is the presence of persuasion in their personalities. Intrusive people can usually give plausible-sounding reasons for feeling as they do. Sometimes this persuasiveness is given through friendly coercion; sometimes it is accompanied by authoritative force. Either way, you may feel like you will create a tug of war if you resist; and being repelled by that prospect, you just comply.

Characteristics of Intrusive People

In order to resist intrusiveness, it will be important to keep your focus on healthy goals for your relationships. You will need to recognize how intrusiveness ultimately will bring harm to you and the relationship because it is accompanied by characteristics that run contradictory to thriving relations. Consider how certain traits tend to be exhibited by intrusive people. For example, you are likely to experience the following:

- Ready invalidation of your perspective as opposed to an ability to assimilate your perspective.
- Poor empathy as opposed to an understanding heart.
- Easy defensiveness as opposed to being open-minded.
- Ready criticism as opposed to seeing what is good.
- Interrupting during conversations as opposed to give-and-take discussions.
- Non-productive uses of anger as opposed to clean assertiveness.
- Use of guilt induction as opposed to allowing free choice.
- Little time awareness as opposed to consideration regarding your schedule.

As you realize that the presence of intrusiveness creates the possibility of many other harmful traits, perhaps you can find motivation to respond in less enabling ways. That is what I hope for people like Jean. By participating in relationship patterns where you do little to disengage from the unhealthiness, you increase the possibilities for emotional duress that will follow you in other areas of your life.

For instance, Jean told me that she felt increasing tension as the weekend approached because that's when Mother had the most opportunities to get between herself and Steve. "Any time I make plans for Saturdays, I'm thinking about what Mother will say about it and how that will affect Steve. I become a bundle of nerves because I don't want to be in the middle. I've *got* to somehow find a way to be stronger."

"Jean, as you consider establishing your stipulations with your mother, it will be helpful for you to remember that you are taking a stand for good traits, not bad ones. By being intrusive, your mother is actually displaying some of her own inner emptiness; so when you choose to separate from her requirements, you are calmly letting her know what you believe is best."

Understand that intrusive people are driven by a large personal reservoir of insecurity. When they push themselves heavily upon others, they are indicating that they fear not being taken seriously. Like anyone else, they have a need to feel significant, but the depth of their pushiness implies that they secretly feel undervalued.

Jean reflected, "You know, I'm at a stage in my adult life where I can stand back and look at my mother more as a regular person. In the past, she was such an imposing figure that I naturally assumed that her opinions were final. Now, though, I am just beginning to give myself permission to see her as more fragile. When she comes on too strong, I'm recognizing that she is actually displaying feelings of weakness."

It was important for Jean to recognize this truth about her mother, not so she could be smug and critical, but so she could sidestep the "invitation" to set aside her own good thinking in order to appease her mother. Being anchored in truth, the subjective (or emotional) aspects of her thinking could be tempered by the objective facts. This would ensure a wiser decision-making process.

To stay out of the clutches of an intrusive person, ask yourself, "Is it my responsibility to make this person feel good about what I do?" The answer is no. It *is* your responsibility to be as considerate and kind as you can, but that is not the same as being required to show universal compliance. When you act right, there is no guarantee that intrusive people will feel good about your decisions. In fact, the opposite is a strong possibility.

A second question to ask of yourself is, "Is it my responsibility to cure this person?" Again, the answer is no. You will want to be available to help others when they attempt to help themselves, but there is no certainty that intrusive people will think they need a cure at all. Some will continue in their pushy ways, oblivious to the reality that they are causing problems. You can drive yourself to great distraction if you make it your job to bring change to a person who feels no need to change.

Choosing Your Own Path

So how can you react when you have people in your life who persist with intrusive behavior? That's the question that Jean was confronted with. I spoke with her about this matter. "Jean, as you decide how you will manage your relationship with your mother, keep in mind that you are ultimately free to choose whatever you think is best. There is no fixed agenda stating how you must act."

"In my mind I know that's the way to approach it," Jean replied, "but it's something I have to remind myself about over and over. I'm so accustomed to responding to Mother in a subservient manner that it will take a little reminder for me to change my reactions."

I tried to add a little extra perspective as I said, "It may sound strange, but I want you to remember that you *can* continue to choose the lousy reactions if that's the way you are inclined. Only when you recognize that your excessive people pleasing is the result of a specific choice can you feel right about possibly making choices in the right direction."

Think about the people in your life who are intrusive. It may be a person at work, your spouse, a child, a neighbor, someone at church, an extended family member. Are you aware that as you respond to their intrusions you are always making a choice? To get an idea of the way to monitor your relations with intrusive people, let's examine your options, then you decide what makes the most sense in your circumstances.

Poor Options

In our reactions to intrusive people, there are some things you can do (I suspect these are things you actually *do*) which will keep you in the cycle of unpleasant relating. Don't say you *can't* do these things. Realize you can . . . and then consider the possible outcomes.

#1. Cater to Them

Easily, the most common choice made by people pleasers regarding intrusive people is to do whatever has to be done to keep them from becoming upset. When persons are overbearing, it is an option for you to determine what is on their agenda and then attempt to do what the agenda says. Let them know, "I will play along with your games."

For instance, Jean told me that she had made a few attempts to go against her mother's grain in her early twenties. "Before I got married I made a major decision not to go to work for someone she had recommended. She had gotten me an interview with a long-time friend and he actually offered me a good job, but I decided that it wasn't for me. My mother tried to pretend that she was OK with my decision, but she wasn't. For a year she would frequently bring up his name and speculate what it might have been like to work for him."

"How did this affect you?"

"You'd think my resolve would have become stronger; but the more she talked about it, the more I told myself that it wasn't worth the price if I disagreed too often with her because she would wear me down with her second-guessing. I've resigned myself to the fact that it's easier just to go along with her so I don't have to listen to her complaints."

Of course, that is exactly what Mother wanted. Jean had decided that catering to her was the path of least resistance, so on the many subsequent occasions when she could have continued being distinct, she instead went along just to get along. As the years passed, Jean's bitterness only increased.

#2. Avoid Them; Be Evasive

Often I hear of people pleasers who go to great lengths to avoid intrusive people because they assume that being direct about their alternative plans will only be painful. As a result, these people can become masters of deceit and cunning. These are not traits they would naturally choose for themselves, yet because they cannot bear to face the barrage of an intruder's unsolicited advice, they become what they do not want to be.

For instance, Jean told me about how excited she was that an old college friend was going to come from out of town to spend the weekend with her. Then she said, "I'm trying hard not to let my mother know that my friend is coming because if she finds out, she'll either try to instruct me about what she would do, or she may even try to tag along with us. This may be rude to say, but I don't want my mother interfering with a wonderful weekend."

To keep her cover, Jean was vague when Mother asked, "Whatcha doing this weekend?" She didn't tell her any lies, but she didn't tell her the truth. She just said, "Oh, I don't have everything decided yet; we'll see what happens."

Evasiveness is a choice, but it is accompanied with less than honest communication.

#3. Try to Force Them to Quit Being Manipulative

Sometimes people pleasers feel emboldened enough to take on intrusive people with a frontal approach. After holding in their anger for long stretches of time, they finally determine that enough is enough, so when the opportunity comes to give the intruder a piece of their minds, they let it fly!

Is it good to be direct toward intrusive people? Yes, it can be *if* it is accomplished without turning the interaction into a war. Since most intrusive people tend to be thin-skinned and forceful, it is highly probable that they will attack when confronted, and that is when the interaction can fall apart quickly.

Jean told me about an incident when her husband, Steve, had a very distasteful exchange with her mother. "She was at the house when Steve came through the kitchen carrying a load of laundry to the washer. I'm always proud of him for doing things like that because not all husbands do. Mother and I were in the kitchen, so when he passed by she proceeded to give him advice about how to handle the laundry. Steve dropped the clothes right there on the floor, whirled around and told her he hadn't asked for her advice and he'd appreciate it if she'd let him mind his own business without her having to butt in."

"Boy, I'll bet that caught her off guard," I remarked.

"It caught us all off guard, including Steve. As soon as he was out of earshot, Mother started in on him, telling me that he had no right to say what he said. I could tell right there that not only did she not hear his sentiment, she now counted him as an enemy."

While intrusive people may not catch on if you confront them with an easy-going style, a forceful approach almost certainly creates more problems than it solves. Intruders tend to think in power terms. That is, they want to be the controller, the most authoritative, the one with the best ideas. When this is challenged forcefully, not only will they not receive what is said, they feel a personal responsibility to neutralize the "opponent."

#4. Talk About Intrusive People Behind Their Backs

Let's recognize that people pleasers are not always happy people. While they may attempt to put on a smile in most circumstances, they can carry plenty of hidden frustration. Since that frustrated emotion cannot stay hidden forever, it will eventually work its way into the open. One of the most common means of managing frustration is talking about the frustrating people behind their backs.

Do you ever complain about intrusive people behind their backs? Have you noticed what can happen to you when you do? First, let's acknowledge that it is not entirely wrong to share your aggravations with a trusted friend. Sometimes it can be good to know that someone else knows your situation and can empathize with your plight. One major problem can emerge, though, if you do too much behind-the-back griping. You can turn into a sour pessimist who takes on a victim's attitude.

Jean confessed that she would often call her sister after an encounter with her mother and the two of them could go on and on about her bad traits. "I noticed that after I hung up the phone, I wouldn't feel better. Actually, I'd be more agitated than ever. It's like those conversations just juiced me up emotionally, but then I had nowhere to go with that emotional energy." This admission illustrated how fruitless complaining can be likened to picking at a scab. Not only might the healing be hindered, but the scar leaves a worse imprint.

Good Options

It can be helpful to examine the poor options for dealing with intrusive people because it can cause you to think more carefully about why you would want to commit to cleaner ways of responding to your problems. There *are* better ways to respond when people push themselves upon you. As we look at some of the better options, remember that you may not succeed in changing the intrusive person, but you *can* succeed in presenting yourself in a way that will lead to more favorable results.

#1. Do What You Know Is Best Without Seeking Approval

People pleasers crave approval, sometimes to the point of addiction. They can convince themselves that they cannot move forward with their good preferences if other people do not back them fully. Intrusive people, however, can be very stingy in the giving of approval, which can create a problem if you *have* to have it. To remove yourself from the debilitating influence of intrusive people, you will need to accept the reality that approval may never come when you act decisively, but that is not your ultimate motivation. You will need to focus instead on what you know is wisest, knowing that you can live with your wise choices even in the absence of outer approval.

Moving forward with your plans may be all the more difficult when you receive scorn, but you will need to reckon to yourself that others cannot have the power of God over you. For instance, Jean talked with me about a decision she was going to make which her mother would surely be angry about. "Steve received a wonderful bonus recently, so we've decided that we're going to upgrade our living room furniture. My parents have always put a heavy emphasis on savings, so when I casually told her about our furniture plans, she went ballistic. She kept trying to make me promise we would put the money into a mutual fund and I kept explaining that we would really like the new furniture. I finally told her I couldn't discuss the matter any more because I didn't want to stay upset. So we dropped the subject. And now that we've been furniture shopping, I almost feel as if I'm doing something dirty or devious."

"Let's put a perspective on this," I mentioned. "I can appreciate her trying to teach good stewardship regarding your money."

Jean quickly interrupted, "Oh, that's never been a problem for me and Steve. We both are frugal with our money and we have excellent savings and retirement accounts."

"Then that makes your case even more clear-cut. You know you're being responsible and you're planning on using the money wisely. Can you determine that you will enjoy the results of your decision even if Mother disapproves?"

"I'm working on it," was Jean's reply. "I've been filtering my decisions through her for so long that it feels odd to be so openly different, but I've got to draw my line. I'm a grown woman with a good mind. Maybe she can't see that, but it's time for me to move forward whether or not she can appreciate what I'm choosing."

Jean was coming to terms with the reality that in many decisions there is not necessarily one absolutely right way to think. Her mother's disapproval did not mean she was wrong. In this case, it only meant that Mother was stubborn. Jean could give herself permission to move forward knowing that her good sense, not Mother's approval, would be the determining factor in the matter.

#2. Explain Your Position Once; Then Drop It

"Jean, I want to ask you something. When you told your mother you and Steve were going to use the money for the furniture, despite her disapproval, how strongly did you feel that you had to give her a good explanation for your decision?"

"*Very* strongly," she replied quickly. "I found myself explaining to her how we'd been faithful in contributing to our retirement accounts and how we had waited until we could pay for our purchases with cash."

"Let me guess. Mother then replied, 'Oh, well, now that you've explained it like that, you have my approval. Proceed as planned.' Is that the way it went?" Of course, she knew I was saying this facetiously, knowing full well it did not play out that way.

"You've got to be kidding. The more I tried to justify my decision, the more she bore down on me. She just can't leave well enough alone."

Sound familiar? In most instances, when you try to satisfy intrusive people with good answers, they take it as an invitation to argue. Instead of hearing you fully, they will find the "holes" in your logic and attack. So this leaves you with one good option: Explain your reasoning one time; then if it is clear that you will only receive arguments, move on with no further explanations.

I explained to Jean, "When you realize she's determined to pick an argument, it can be reasonable for you to simply state, 'Well, that's the decision I've made.' Then say no more."

"But what if she keeps on pushing her point?"

"Calmly repeat, 'That is the decision I've made.' Then once again become silent. You're not obliged to spar with her."

Accept a simple truth: Intrusive people have to be right, and anything that differs from their logic is automatically wrong. Nothing short of full agreement will please them, but you can accept another truth: you have a good mind. God gave you the privilege to use your reasoning in confronting your daily circumstances. You get to use that good mind even if another person deems it wrong. Be wise enough to weigh what others say, then exercise your freedom to move forward with what you believe.

#3. Exact Consequences If Necessary

One of the most difficult, yet necessary, steps to take with intrusive people is establishing consequences. In child rearing, for instance, when children disobey, they can be trained to make more mature choices by experiencing consequences for their wrongs. Parents are not mean when they give consequences (despite the children's potential protests), but this is part of a loving approach. Consequences teach, and that is the purpose of discipline.

Sometimes adults need to be taught via consequences just as children do. As an example, if you speed on the highway, you could receive a citation, which would then teach you to slow down. People pleasers hesitate to see themselves in the role of teacher toward intrusive people, but indeed that can be a necessary role to take on. In all that you do, you are educating others regarding the way they can treat you. I explained to Jean, "You may not realize it, but your mother is taking cues from you regarding what you will accept from her. When you acquiesce to her strong commands, you can be sending the message, 'Go ahead and walk on me because I'll take it.'"

"I never thought about it that way, but I can see that's exactly what she reads from me."

"Without being harsh or condescending, you may need to pick some circumstances to set consequences so you will teach her what you can live with and what you cannot."

Jean later told me that she hired a baby-sitter one summer day to stay with Seth while she had a doctor's appointment. When her mother learned of this and asked why she had not been called first, Jean explained, "The last couple of times you watched Seth for me, you went counter to what I had asked and you let him do some things I specifically didn't want him to do, so this time I decided to call a baby-sitter to help me instead." The mother was stunned, but Jean had made her point.

"It was hard to be that frank with her, but I had to communicate that I wanted her to take my parenting decisions more seriously. I think she'll listen better the next time, but if she doesn't, I'll let her experience another consequence."

Your circumstances will vary, of course, from Jean's, but you too may need to educate others who will not listen to your words. By acting upon your principles in ways that demonstrate you will not tolerate disrespect, others can eventually learn to make more appropriate choices.

#4. Remove Yourself from Their Influence

There are times when intrusive people can be so oblivious to others' feelings or needs that nothing short of separation will stop the struggle. This is not desirable, yet it may be the last option left for you as you try to maintain your emotional composure.

Fortunately for Jean, she did not have to go so far with her mother that she had to separate from her, but she told me about an earlier incident involving a neighbor who just could not be trusted. "I made friends with her knowing she needed the influence of a solid Christian family. I knew she'd struggled to find balance with both her husband and her kids. She was constantly at odds with them, so I wanted to be a good sounding board. Unfortunately, as I got to know her, she became very demanding of my time and when I would try to set boundaries, she'd act highly offended. Finally, I just quit calling her and she got the message and quit calling me."

Was Jean wrong to step away from this woman? Not really. It is regrettable, yet true, that some people will remain committed to their controlling and intrusive behavior no matter how much damage it inflicts. With low levels of personal insight, they will probably blame their relationship woes on everyone else, never taking responsibility upon themselves for the problems they repeatedly experience. When you are faced with such oblivion, you may need to move on to healthier ways to spend your time, not because you want to be rejecting, but because you need to experience healthiness.

People pleasers like Jean will come to terms with intrusive people only when they remember that they have options and they select the options most consistent with good relationship parameters. You can expect that the intrusive people will not always understand the boundaries or stipulations you espouse, yet forcing understanding upon these folks is not the goal. Living in accordance to solid character traits is the goal.

In the last chapter, we will examine what some of those solid character traits are, and you will be challenged to fix your minds upon successful qualities rather than getting pulled into patterns that bring you down.

For Personal Reflection

In what ways do people act intrusively with you?

_____

_____

_____

_____

How do they seem to justify their intrusions, even though it may be clear that their reasoning is flawed?

_____

_____

What insecurities lie behind the intrusiveness of people that demand your attention?

Catering to intrusive people is an option. Why is this not a good one?

In what ways might you encounter resistance as you try to get away from the grip of intrusiveness?

It can be wise to proceed with choices you know are good despite intrusive people's protests. Why might this be difficult for you?

When might it be necessary for you to enact consequences with an intrusive person? What would those consequences be?

_____

_____

_____

_____

In what circumstances might it be best to remove yourself from an intrusive person's influence?

_____

_____

_____

_____

Chapter 12

Traits of a Healthy Relationship

A t times in my counseling practice, I am thrust into the role of a coach, teaching individuals how to successfully apply traits that will profit them in their relationships. For instance, with an anxious person, I might coach calm inner confidence. With an angry person, I may coach a patient and accepting spirit. With a depressed person, I may coach openness. Part of the healing process is the identification of healthy traits with the intent of making those traits integral to the lifestyle.

When I work with chronic people pleasers, I often feel like we are beginning a step or two ahead of the rest of the crowd. Most people pleasers have dedicated themselves to genuinely good traits and they are quite conscientious about projecting an image of kindness or concern. In the midst of all her difficulties with her mother, for instance, Jean told me that her childhood training consisted of special emphasis in the fruit of the Spirit: love, joy, peace, patience, kindness, goodness, faithfulness, gentleness, and self-control. "We had a neat wall-hanging in our kitchen that listed those traits along with a poetic description of each one. It was beautifully done in calligraphy and was something I read over and over. I know my mother can get on my nerves a lot, but I've got to give her credit for trying to teach godliness."

183

Jean, like so many others of her kind, did not need coaching regarding the positive relationship traits. If anything, she was over-trained in the gentle qualities. Instead, she needed a more balanced understanding of how to use those healthy traits without also suc-cumbing to the demanding styles of others. Being godly does not require a person to become a doormat. To the contrary, there is noth-ing righteous in being pleasant while simultaneously playing along with unhealthy relationship patterns.

As I work with people pleasers, I find it helpful to focus on four key personal ingredients which can keep them in their loving mode, yet, when properly balanced, can also prevent them from experiencing distresses associated with dysfunctional relating patterns. Those ingre-dients are respect, empathy, objectivity, and confidence. I teach them to realize how these traits do contribute to relational success but *do not* require unnecessary acquiescence to people who might have less than pure motives.

To get an idea how you can integrate these traits into your relating style, let's examine each one with the goal of applying balance in your gracious spirit.

Respect

Think of Robert, the dentist who wanted to please his patients and his staff to the extent that he felt like he was underappreciated in his efforts. Sometimes, despite his kindness toward patients, he would still receive petty complaints, and sometimes when he made conces-sions to his staff's needs, he felt like they didn't reciprocate the same spirit. "I try to be respectful to people across the board, but it doesn't always turn out the way it should," he explained. "I wonder if it makes people think they can take advantage of my good nature because they know that I'm not the type of person who will fly off the handle when I am disappointed."

Can you relate to Robert's situation? Have you ever felt that you have truly attempted to show respect, only to find that someone stepped on you anyway? To get an idea of how respect works, let's consider what it is and what it is not.

Respect can be defined as a caring concern and an unconditional regard for others. Specifically, as you give respect, you are openly acknowledging others' God-given worth. Respect prompts you to treat others as you would prefer to be treated. It includes communication toward others as one equal to another. Some people operate with the mistaken assumption that respect should first be earned, when in fact it can be given even in circumstances when it does not seem merited. (Consider, for instance, a family member who has angered you. Though you may strongly dislike what was done, you can still choose to handle your transactions with that person respectfully.)

Following are some behaviors that flow from an attitude of respect.

- Speaking in an even tone of voice during a disagreement.
- Finding what is right about a person and commenting on that.
- Listening carefully during a disagreement, realizing you could learn something from a differing point of view.
- Being kind even when it is not required.
- Remembering little things about another person's preferences or needs.
- Speaking well about someone when in the presence of others.
- Choosing not to be critical or insulting when the opportunity presents itself.
- Making room for the fact that others are imperfect, showing acceptance.
- Choosing not to participate in behind-the-back gossip about someone.
- Being known as fair-handed in the way you deal with people.

As you commit to the characteristic of respect, you demonstrate a commitment toward positive contributions in relationships. Your respectfulness demonstrates an understanding that people are motivated best when they know they are highly regarded. The Bible teaches, "Let each of us please his neighbor for his good, to his edification" (Rom. 15:2). Scripture shows that people are most influential when they are an ongoing uplifting presence in the lives of others.

Robert told me, "What you teach about respect is exactly what I believe. I know I need to do a better job of listening during disagreements, and sometimes my impatience with a job can cause me to be a little abrupt. But as a general rule, I think I do a fairly decent job trying to treat people with dignity." Then sighing, he mentioned, "I tend to lose my motivation when I realize that my commitment toward respect is just a one-way street."

He then gave me an illustration about how he had given his office manager, Melissa, great latitude in the way she handled business affairs, yet he had a growing feeling that she forgot who the boss really was. "When I hired her, we spent a lot of time those first weeks going over my office procedures. We were very specific in spelling out goals regarding the ways employees would be handled, how patients would be treated, how insurance would be managed. As office manager she had a lot to juggle, so I wanted her to feel like she had my full attention and support. Once we established the broad parameters, I backed away and let her set her own style and pace. I didn't want to be known as an intrusive boss.

"As time has passed," Robert continued, "I have felt like Melissa has strayed from some of our early agreements. In particular, she can be aloof toward employees she doesn't really like, and she's gaining a reputation for playing favorites. What's worse, when I have input to give regarding a business matter, she seems easily offended. She's got thin skin and seems to resent my having an opinion. Here I am, a boss who actively tries to treat my employees right and I get this kind of treatment in return. It makes me wonder if my good guy image is actually enabling her attitude."

Chances are, you have felt similar frustrations in the roles you play, whether it is as an employee, parent, spouse, or friend. You know the emptiness of being respectful toward others without getting much in return. So what can you do?

First, it is necessary to recognize what respect is *not*. Respect is not the same as condoning wrong behaviors or attitudes of others. It does not require you to let go of your firm convictions, nor does it mean you are giving positive reinforcement to people acting counter to your beliefs. Sometimes, people pleasers assume that respectfulness necessitates that they maintain a non-committal attitude toward things that are not good, but that is not at all the case.

Respect can be given even in situations that are negatively charged; yet you can still take a stand for what you know is best or right. For instance, after much thought, Robert decided he needed to have a meeting with his office manager, Melissa, for the purpose of redefining her role. He explained to me, "I told her that I appreciated her high commitment to excellence and that I believed she was doing a good job. Then I explained the importance of receiving input from all employees, including myself, regarding the various functions of running an office. I mentioned that it was important to me that she put as much initiative as possible into being an encourager, given the high-profile position that she maintained. I think I did a good job of holding my ground while also maintaining a positive regard for her throughout our meeting."

Do you recognize what Robert did in this confrontation? He upheld the dignity of Melissa even as he addressed an uncomfortable situation. In the meantime, he also maintained respect for his own legitimate needs. He was recognizing that when he gave others the gift of respect, it did not mean he had to simultaneously show disrespect toward himself, a common mistake among people pleasers.

As you continue to incorporate respect into your interactive patterns, you can still allow yourself to think and prioritize firmly. You need not feel that it is your job to make the other person feel that you agree with all that they think or do. Nonetheless, you can establish that, *even as you address differences,* civility and courtesy can remain in place.

Empathy

When I counsel people with troubled relationships, a key ingredient almost always lacking is empathy. While good relationships are characterized by large doses of understanding and patience, the troubled ones are typified by a lack of listening and by an inability to factor in the perspectives of another person. Teamwork, then, is what I seek to introduce to those relationships, and empathy is the quality that makes it happen.

Empathy is defined as the ability to experience the emotions and perceptions of others to the extent that a powerful understanding of others' perspectives occurs. At the moment you empathize, you are stepping away from your own self-focus for the purpose of being more fully attuned to the perspectives of others. As we explored in an earlier chapter, humility can take over your relational style, and you can acknowledge that just as you yearn to feel understood, so does the other person. You can give what you would hope to receive.

Often, people pleasers are very conscientious about the emotional disposition of others. In fact, sometimes they can be so keenly aware of the feelings of others that they feed off of others' emotions too powerfully. Being easily sucked in by others' emotions, however, does not necessarily make a person a good empathizer. True empathy is a positive addition to your relational skills, not a negative.

Let's go back to Eilene, the now-single woman who had capitulated for years under the burden of trying to please her controlling ex-husband, Walt. "I've always had a sixth sense for a person's emotional state," she said. "In fact, if anything, I think I was too empathetic. I would be so caught up in what others felt that I'd base my decisions on that."

Was Eilene describing empathy? Not really. She was describing how her dependent state of mind kept her from moving forward with good relational skills. Just because she was highly affected by emotionally charged circumstances, we can't say she was being empathetic.

To get an idea of how empathy can be a tremendous asset to your relating style, look over the following ways it could affect your relationships.

- When someone tells you about a day's twisted schedule, you could respond with, "This must have been one of those days when everything went haywire. Wow! I'll bet you had your share of aggravations."

- When a coworker is unusually upbeat after hanging up the phone, you might comment, "Looks like that problem you were worried about is going to be handled after all. What a load off your shoulders that must be."
- If a friend becomes saddened as she tells you about a very disappointing experience, you can put your hand on her shoulder and say, "Just know that I want to hear your needs because I can tell this is weighing heavily on you."
- When a child gripes because he can't keep the weekend plans he wants, you can say, "I know you're frustrated when things don't go as you hoped. It's a big disappointment."

Empathy is shown when you are able to read the "insides" of others and you can communicate that you are aware of what they are experiencing. Empathy does *not* mean that you necessarily agree with what the other person feels nor does it show a softness in you that becomes an invitation to be overwhelmed. It simply means that you have a discernment about the other person's state of mind.

I explained to Eilene that empathy might have helped her in dealing with Walt's frequent foul moods. For instance, if he was angry because she had spent money he didn't want her to spend, she could mentally enter his thinking: "For his whole life he's worried that he wouldn't have enough. Sometimes that uncertainty can create some real tension in him." She could feel with him about his experiences, and it would help her determine more accurately how she would then respond. It didn't necessarily mean she agreed with his assessment of her but that she was just trying to get a feel regarding the motivation behind his words. (Usually when Walt griped, she was so busy thinking of how she would defend herself, that she could not truly empathize).

Once I explained empathy to her, I then mentioned, "There is another trait that you will also need in order to keep your empathy balanced. That's the trait objectivity." Let's examine how this can be a necessary part of successful relating.

Objectivity

If empathy causes you to enter into the subjective experiences of others, objectivity keeps you from getting so emotionally pulled in that you lose your ability to manage your needs appropriately. Objectivity happens when you are uninfluenced by emotions to the extent that you can maintain a mindset of logic and fairness. While empathy helps you to maintain a keen sensitivity to others' "behind the scenes" issues, objectivity keeps you focused nonetheless on the values you hold and the lifestyle goals that you know are best. Understand that objectivity and empathy are not opposites to each other; rather, they provide balance to each other.

Suppose, for example, that you are asked by a friend to help on a matter that you have neither the expertise needed nor the time to pursue it. You can be empathetic: "As I hear you describe the complexity of the problem, I can imagine that it creates major stress as you try to figure out how best to tackle it." You can also express objectivity: "I'm not the right person to be assisting you on this project. I'm not familiar enough with the subject, nor does my schedule allow it." The balance is demonstrated as you are attuned to the emotions while sticking to the facts.

Taking it one step further, suppose the friend pushes the point and persists with the request anyway. You can still use both traits: "You really do feel a sense of urgency in this project" followed by "Nonetheless, I'm still not the person for this job." Even as the other person's emotions may change or intensify, the facts remain the same. Objective people are able to step away from the subjective tugging and stick to logic.

Eilene remarked, "I *wish* that I had the ability to think like that, but I am so driven by the mood of the moment that I don't let objectivity have its final say. I get suckered into all sorts of matters against my better judgment because I let my emotions rule."

"Let's not be too hasty in assuming you can't think that way," I replied. "Objectivity may not be the most natural trait for you *yet,* but it can happen." I then explained that when her experiences of getting sucked into excessive people pleasing were sufficiently painful, she would develop the motivation to sustain objectivity.

"If pain is a motivator for better objectivity, then I should be ready," she replied with a nervous chuckle. I agreed because I knew she had been through more pain than she needed.

People pleasers, being easily motivated by all sorts of emotions, find objectivity difficult for one major reason. While objectivity implies that one person can only go so far in helping others solve their problems, people pleasers feel badly if they see others struggling to find emotional balance. They assume it is their responsibility to take on others' emotional baggage when, in fact, it is not. Their emotions want to rewrite hard facts.

When you choose to hold firmly to objectivity, though, you will find your relating style to be positively affected. For instance:

- If someone feels badly about a problem he brought on himself, you can feel badly with him while also realizing that you are limited in your ability to make the problem go away.
- You can let others have their anger without always assuming it is you who caused the anger.
- When a person experiences an unexpected positive event, you can be glad for her; yet you don't have to get pulled into envy because the same didn't happen to you.
- When a relative rejects you, you can weigh the facts first to determine just how much responsibility you should accept for the rejection.
- If a child or a subordinate goes counter to you, recognize that this happens to many other people. You can calmly state consequences without being overly agitated.
- When you make mistakes, you can admit the truth: You're a mistake-maker. You will take on no more shame than the situation warrants.
- During a disagreement, if the other person gets overly excited, you can remind yourself that it does no good to let your emotions get carried away, too. You'll respond with an even tone of voice.

- When someone tries to manipulate you into his schemes, you can determine your course of action by considering first what you believe is consistent with your priorities.

Respect and empathy keep you in the portion of your personality that is most satisfying and pleasing toward others. When objectivity is added into the mix, you can trust yourself to be more consistent in keeping relationship boundaries even in the midst of your pleasant efforts. So, ask yourself: When I am kind and giving, what facts do I tend to ignore? Perhaps you'll recognize that you could more accurately factor in the truth that you cannot be everyone else's hero, nor can you mend every person's distasteful emotions.

In Eilene's case, for instance, she learned to recognize that Walt had a problem with a critical spirit. That was simply a fact. It was also a fact that he would continue in this mode regardless of her efforts to remake herself into his liking. Knowing this as objective truth, she could determine for herself how she would prefer to live when Walt or someone like him persisted in being critical. The facts indicated that placation would be a poor choice because it only fed the other person's feeling of power. She began realizing that despite the critical person's desire to control, she could still make the choices she deemed appropriate. It was up to her to weigh the facts, especially in the moments when her emotions tried to sway her to act in self-damaging ways.

Confidence

None of the traits that are part of thriving relationships can be sustained long without a solid foundation of confidence. Rather than interacting with an undertow of self-doubt, you will need to proceed with the realization that you are capable of good skills and you have the strength to live with those skills leading the way. Confidence, then, can be defined as faith in your own ability to handle circumstances with appropriateness and discernment.

Jean spoke with me about a problem common to many people pleasers. "In my private moments, I can analyze a problem and I have a feeling of security because I know that my reasoning is sound. But later, I can be around someone strong-willed, like my mother, and my inner strength seems to dissolve. I don't know why my faith in myself can be so easily shaken."

"Do you find that this trend plays out with other people beyond just your mother?"

"Yes. In the past, I used to be a buyer for a furniture store. It was a great business for me because it held my interest so well. But there were times when I'd buckle if someone came on real strong. It's like I've been trained to set aside my good thinking if someone more powerful than I comes along."

Jean may not have realized it, but her statement was right on target. She had been trained early to have less confidence in her own opinions than in others'. As a girl, she had needed regular encouragement to run with her own ideas, even if it meant making mistakes. She needed someone to ask often, "What do you think?" or "Let me get your input on this." Instead, she received a lot of advice she did not want and she was told how to feel and behave. Now as an adult, when her opinions were on the line, she did not possess the confidence to stick with her perspectives.

How can a person like Jean find confidence when it was not adequately trained in the early developmental years? First, she needed to recognize that the lack of training did not mean she had a lack of capability. She had demonstrated that she had good common sense, so she could afford to be more firm in standing her ground. Second, she needed to recognize that others' lack of confidence in her decisions did not necessarily reflect badly on her. It could just as easily be interpreted to mean that the other persons had their own insecurities to confront, or perhaps they were pridefully controlling.

I remarked to Jean, "As I've gotten to know you, I've realized that you are not at all harsh in your beliefs nor are you the kind of person to be uncooperative as you learn about the needs or desires of others. You've got a genuinely pleasant spirit."

"Well, I hope that you're not the only one who sees that," she replied. "I feel like I try hard to be fair in my relationships. Maybe my mother doesn't fully appreciate it, but I'm very loyal to her, and I really do consider her needs as I make the decisions I make."

"That being the case," I explained, "let me encourage you to become anchored in a major notion. You need to interact with her with the belief that you have good things to offer. Not that you're going to start acting puffed up, but you bring good perspectives to the table that your mother needs to hear. As you stand firmly on your own belief in yourself, it may cause her to rethink her willingness to take you more seriously."

Confidence is based on the very real belief that your ideas or perspectives are legitimate. Do you believe that about yourself? As confidence becomes more foundational in your thinking, you will notice a very real effect on your behaviors. For instance:

- You will not automatically shut down your initiatives just because they are questioned.
- Others will be allowed to have erratic reactions to you, but you can still proceed in the knowledge that those reactions may be less about you and more about the persons having them.
- You can take hesitancy out of your voice inflections, speaking with calm assuredness.
- You will have no need to "sell" your ideas to others. You can stand firmly on what you know is best.
- You can interpret your own differences from others as being just that—different. This does not mean you are better or worse, but unique.
- You can give yourself permission to go with your "gut instincts." It could be that you will find that your notions are trustworthy.
- You will stay out of debates, not because you are afraid to debate, but because you know that you don't always have to "prove" that you are OK.

My desire for people like Jean or Eilene or Robert is that they can build upon the realization that conflict does not always indicate that they have erred and should therefore drop their valid ideas. When you know that you are being as fair and balanced as you can, that is something to create inner peace in you. People pleasing often represents a futile attempt to be affirmed by those who won't affirm, no matter what you do. Confidence allows you to be exactly what your circumstances need you to be and pleasing others becomes secondary to being appropriate.

As you ponder the adjustments that can bring your pleasing behavior into balance, consider the benefits of a life of calm assertiveness versus unbalanced people pleasing:

Imbalanced People Pleasing	Calm Assertiveness
1. Encourages others to take advantage of you in disrespectful ways	1. Encourages others to see you as a person with dignity
2. Plays into the self-serving schemes of others	2. Tries to get others to see the reality of teamwork
3. Allows false guilt or fear to be a motivator for behavior	3. Allows fair-mindedness to be a motivator for behavior
4. Permits your direction to be based on reactions to others	4. Permits your direction to be based on well-conceived initiatives
5. Demonstrates emotions are suppressed	5. Demonstrates emotions can be properly expressed
6. Leads to feelings of burnout	6. Leads to feelings of fulfillment
7. Tries to take responsibility for others' happiness	7. Realizes that others are ultimately responsible for their own happiness
8. Lives with a walking-on-eggshells feeling toward others	8. Lives with openness and self-acceptance
9. Becomes an appeaser when others are angry	9. Can objectively weigh the facts when others are angry
10. Won't stand up for convictions in the presence of overpowering people	10. Realizes the responsibility of standing up for convictions

Are you up to the task? I have written this book with the intent of showing you that you need not filter your every decision through others' grids. Yes, it is good to be keenly aware of others' legitimate needs, just as it is good to consider how your decisions affect their quality of life. Simultaneously, though, you will need to recognize that others have flaws and imperfections that they cannot amend if you constantly seek to appease them even as they live insensitively. Being firm in what you know is right or best may not *feel* comfortable at the moment, but long-term healthiness can become a higher priority to you than short-term discomfort.

For Personal Reflection

In what ways have you been respectful to others only to have them be disrespectful to you in return?

_____

_____

_____

_____

In what situations could you do a better job of displaying both respect and firmness at the same time?

_____

_____

_____

_____

_____

In what circumstances are you most skilled in being empathetic?

_____

_____

_____

_____

When do others view your understanding nature as an invitation to be insensitive?

_____

_____

_____

_____

_____

How might objectivity serve as a balance to empathy?

_____

_____

_____

_____

_____

When do you need to respond to people by letting facts, not emotions, determine your course of action?

_____

_____

_____

_____

_____

In what ways do people seem to rob you of your confidence?

_____

_____

_____

_____

Suppose you are in the presence of a strong-willed person who debates and invalidates easily. In what way would you need to apply confidence, as opposed to merely collapsing?

———————————————————————————————

———————————————————————————————

———————————————————————————————

———————————————————————————————

———————————————————————————————

About the Author

Dr. Les Carter maintains an active counseling practice at the Minirth Clinic in Richardson, Texas, where he has been since 1980. He specializes in the treatment of emotional and relational disorders and for years has conducted the popular Anger Workshop and the Boundaries Workshop. He has authored fifteen other books, including the best-selling *Anger Workbook, The Choosing to Forgive Workbook,* and *The Significance Principle.* He is a popular speaker and has conducted seminars in churches and businesses across America.

Dr. Carter is married and has a teenage daughter.